A Guide To The
ORKNEY ISLANDS

Edited, Compiled and Illustrated

by

Gordon Wright

GORDON WRIGHT PUBLISHING
25 MAYFIELD ROAD, EDINBURGH EH9 2NQ
SCOTLAND

ISBN 0 903065 67 3

Illustration of the Maes Howe Dragon on the title page reproduced by kind permission of Ola Gorie Orkney Jewellery.

Cover photograph of Stromness Harbour by Gordon Wright.

Other Orkney books from Gordon Wright Publishing Ltd.

Orkney From Old Photographs: Gordon Wright
Recipes From The Orkney Islands: Eileen Wolfe
Under Brinkie's Brae: George Mackay Brown

The publisher acknowledges the financial assistance of the Orkney Islands Council in the publication of this book.

Typeset by Jo Kennedy.
Printed by Scotprint, Musselburgh, Scotland.

Contents

Where to Find it

Emergency Services: Tel. 999.
Police: Kirkwall (0856) 2241; Stromness (0856) 850222; Longhope (Hoy) 222.
Weather reports: Orkney Met. office: Tel. Kirkwall (0856) 3802.

TRANSPORT
British Airways: Kirkwall Airport: Tel. (0856) 2233.
Loganair: Kirkwall Airport: Tel. (0856) 3457. Charters Tel. (0856) 2420.
P & O Ferries: Pierhead, Stromness. Tel. (0856) 850655 and Harbour St., Kirkwall.
Tel. (0856) 3330. (2 hrs. car and passenger ferry from Scrabster to Stromness).
Orkney Ferries p.l.c. (45 mins. car and passenger ferry between Gills Bay, Canisbay,
Caithness and Burwick, S. Ronaldsay). Burwick Terminal Tel. (0856) 83343.
Thomas & Bews (45 mins. passenger ferry between John o' Groats and Burwick,
South Ronaldsay). Ferry Office, Tel. (095581) 353 or (084785) 619.
Orkney Islands Shipping Co.: 4 Ayre Rd., Kirkwall. Tel. (0856) 2044. Houton
Ferry for the South Isles. Tel. (0856) 81397. Tingwall Ferry for Rousay, Egilsay and
Wyre. Tel. (0856) 75360. Kirkwall / Shapinsay ferry: Tel. (0856) 2044.
Mr. Mowat: Stromness / Hoy Ferry. Tel. (0856) 850624.

ORGANISATIONS
Tourist Information Office: Broad St., Kirkwall. Tel. (0856) 2856. Pierhead,
Stromness, Tel. (0856) 850716.
Consumer Protection Dept.: Council Offices, Kirkwall. Tel. (0856) 3535.
Legal Aid: 5 Broad St., Kirkwall. Tel. (0856) 3151.
Voluntary Services Orkney: Anchor Buildings, 6 Bridge St., Kirkwall. Tel. (0856)
2897. General information on the voluntary sector.
B.B.C. Radio Orkney: Castle St., Kirkwall. Tel. (0856) 3939.
'The Orcadian' (Weekly on Thurs.) 9 Victoria St., Kirkwall. Tel. (0856) 3249.
'Orkney View' (bi-monthly magazine) 3 Papdale Close, Kirkwall. Tel. (0856) 4030.

MEDICAL SERVICES
Doctors: Kirkwall Health Centre, Hospitals and Orkney Health Board. Tel. (0856)
2763. Stromness Health Centre. Tel. (0856) 850205.
Chemists: Boots the Chemist Ltd., 53 Albert St. Kirkwall. Tel. (0856) 2097.
W.H.B. Sutherland Ltd., 31 Victoria St., Kirkwall. Tel. (0856) 3240 and at 74
Victoria St., Stromness. Tel. (0856) 850338.
Dentists: The Strynd Dental Centre, Kirkwall. Tel. (0856) 2958.
Opticians: Bryan Clark, 9-11 Mounthoolie Lane, Kirkwall. Tel. (0856) 2857.

CAMP AND CARAVAN SITES
Kirkwall: Pickaquoy Rd., Kirkwall. Bookings to Orkney Islands Council Education
Dept., Council Offices, Kirkwall KW15.1NY. Tel. (0856) 3535 Ext. 2409.
Stromness: Ness Point Caravan and Camping site. Bookings as above.

HOSTELS AND OUTDOOR CENTRES
Kirkwall: Old Scapa Rd., Orkney KW15.1BB. Tel. (0856) 2243. (Grade 2.) 100
beds. Open 15 May - 1 Oct. Advance bookings S.Y.H.A. Tel. (0786) 51181.
Stromness: Helliehole Rd., Orkney KW16.3DE. Tel. (0856) 850589 (Grade 2.) 40
beds. Open 24 March - 1 Oct. Advance bookings S.Y.H.A. Tel. (0786) 51181.
Birsay: Birsay Outdoor Centre: Oxtro, Birsay, Orkney Mainland. (Grade 2.) 30 beds.
Open all year. Groups only. Bookings to O.I.C. Education Dept. as above.
Island of Hoy: Hoy Outdoor Centre, Orgill, Orkney KW16.3NJ. (Grade 2.) 26 beds.
Open 15 May -12 Sept. Rackwick Outdoor Centre, Hoy, Orkney KW16.3NJ. (Grade
2.) 8 beds. Open 17 March - 12 Sept. Bookings to O.I.C. Education Dept., as above.
Island of Papa Westray: Bookings to Papa Westray Community Co-op, Beltane
House, Papa Westray, Orkney KW17.2BU. Tel. (08574) 267. (Grade 1.) 16 beds.
Open all year.
Island of Eday: Eday Hostel, London Bay. (Grade 3.) 12 beds. Open 24 March to 1
Oct. Bookings to Eday Community Enterprises, Island of Eday, Orkney KW17.2AB.
Tel. (08572) 283.

Introduction

George Mackay Brown

Orkney is a group of islands lying to the north-east of Scotland, beyond Caithness and the Highlands.

One must not think of barren rocks that only seabirds, smugglers, and shipwrecked mariners visit.

It has a long continuous history: written records going back to the medieval Norsemen who settled the islands—records in stone going much further back, megalithic rings and early Celtic forts and Stone Age burial chambers.

Nor did that continuous line of inhabitants live frugally on fish and seabirds. They took pains to cultivate the land, as the generations broke, wave after wave; so that today, a newcomer's first impressions are of greenness and fertility.

Early Celts, Picts, Norsemen, Scots: the modern Orcadian is a mingled weave, and still new threads are being set in the loom—many English families have settled here in the past twenty years. Before that, two World Wars brought new blood into Orkney. Through many centuries, shipwreck has added its salt drop or two. (There are rumours of a Spanish Armada ship wrecked on a north isle).

Undoubtedly the high peak of this rich history was the Norse settlement that began in the ninth or tenth century possibly and lasted for a few hundred years. In those days—a thousand years ago—the power of the Earls of Orkney extended deep into Scotland and the west; the Earl was at least as powerful as the Scottish king. An Orkney earl died fighting in the great Battle at Clontarf near Dublin in 1014. Another, Thorfinn, 'ruled nine earldoms'. Another earl became St. Magnus the Martyr, whose cathedral, begun in Kirkwall in 1137, twenty years after Magnus' death, is still 'the wonder and glory of all the North'. Another earl, Rognvald the Second, made an epic pilgrimage to Jerusalem, Byzantium and Rome—he was also a poet and a man of great charm and ability.

All those magnificent actions are recorded in the medieval *The Orkneyinga Saga*.

Orkney was gradually drawn into the orbit of Scotland; and after that most of the glory departed. A mighty medieval earldom shrank to the status of a minor Scottish county. The pomp and the heraldry and the poetry were lost.

In the twilight of the centuries of Scottish rule, a few characters and events appear murkily—the Stewart earls of the sixteenth and seventeenth centuries, battle and skirmish, tales of learned and eccentric ministers, of the lairds, of smugglers, of merchants, of young men trying to escape from the net of the Press Gang.

Many agricultural improvements took place in the nineteenth century; at last the crofters and small farmers owned their land, and they proved themselves to be industrious 'keepers of the door of corn'—so that today Orkney is a prosperous agricultural community, and the whole of Orkney's economy is based on that fertility.

Fishing, too, is much better organised and more profitable than it was in the past.

What will the modern tourist find? He will find a group of islands 'like sleeping whales', only they are green with the colour of tilth and pasture. Only one island, Hoy, seems like a piece of the Highlands in its northern part; perhaps Hoy keeps the rarest jewel in all Orkney, the island valley of Rackwick, recently threatened with near-depopulation, now showing a healthy upward graph in its population.

There is the town of Kirkwall built round St. Magnus Cathedral; nowadays

The cliffs at Yesnaby

the market and administrative centre of Orkney. On the western side of the main island is the other town, Stromness, that grew rapidly into a seaport in the eighteenth century. There are a dozen or so villages and hamlets, some of them beautiful.

Trout lochs lie everywhere, and the fishing is free.

Orkney attracts archaeologists and lovers of nature from all over the world. Who has not heard of Skara Brae, or Maeshowe, the burial chamber with the one midwinter sun-splash?

The undulant almost treeless landscape is very beautiful, with its hardly ebbing sun in summer, and the dark loud blaze of winter (from stars and gales and snow).

The hills—except Hoy—are quiet and gentle, but all down the west of Orkney, from Westray to Hoy, is an immense battlement of cliffs, with pastoral breaches here and there. To see Yesnaby in a westerly gale, for example, is an unforgetable experience. And always, slowly, the immense power of the Atlantic batters down this bastion and that battlement of crag.

An Orcadian does not like to discuss his own people in print. Let the visitors judge. Perhaps the twentieth century is touching our old ways with its cold impersonality. But there is a lingering kindness and courtesy here and there that impress even a native. A child born and brought up in Stromness, the earliest impressions I had of an innate goodness in people came from rare visits to farms in the country; all was gentleness and generosity. That good kind of life—beautifully recorded in Edwin Muir's *Autobiography*—has not died out by any means.

In this century Orkney has burgeoned with art and literature; and still those crafts proliferate. Perhaps the spirit of the saga-men, and those who built the brochs and kirks and long-ships and crofts, has never really died out; there was only a kind of centuries-long hibernation.

Hardly any visitor to Orkney goes away disappointed, though there may be days of rain and wind and gray skies. Stevenson's great lyric that has those lines, 'Blows the wind today, and the sun and the rain are flying . . . Standing stones on the vacant wine-red moor . . . the howes of the silent vanished races . . .' might almost describe a typical Orkney day.

But there are days too, even in winter, of a rare luminous tranquillity, such as Wordsworth knew walking with a child on another shore: 'quiet as a nun . . .'

Calendar of Events

JANUARY: New Year's Day Ba': Kirkwall. County Ploughing Match. Inter-County Squash: Orkney v. Caithness.

FEBRUARY: SCDA Drama Festival. Light Opera: Kirkwall Amateur Operatic Society. Ploughing Matches. Opening of the sea trout fishing season (25 Feb.). Inter-County Squash: Orkney v. Shetland.

MARCH: Opening of the brown trout fishing season (15 March). Bulb Show: Kirkwall. West Mainland Strathspey & Reel Society concert in Stromness. Orkney Cross-Country Open Championship. Orkney Open Squash Championships: Kirkwall.

APRIL: Tankerness House Museum Exhibition. Stromness Museum Exhibition.

MAY: Balfour Castle tours start on the Island of Shapinsay. Orkney Motorcross Club: Championship points meeting. 'Open Week' Exhibition of local artists at the Pier Arts Centre, Stromness. Orkney Traditional Folk Festival: Stromness and West Mainland. Inter-County Cricket: Orkney v. Shetland.

JUNE: North Isles Sports Day: Stronsay, Sanday or Westray. St. Magnus Festival: Kirkwall and Stromness. Major Festival Art Exhibition at Stromness. Junior County Sports: Orkney v. Shetland. Hoy Marathon. Finstown Gala Day and Regatta. Orkney Golf Championship. Festival of Male Voice Praise: Kirkwall. Midnight bowls, golf & trout fishing on the longest day.

JULY: Haig Shield Sea Angling Competition. P & O Ferries Sea Angling Festival. British Legion Float and Fancy Dress Parade: Kirkwall. Regattas at Stromness, Rousay & Wyre, Burray & South Ronaldsay, Westray, Holm & Longhope. Exhibition of Orkney Crafts: Kirkwall. Stromness Shopping Week (third week). SWRI Handicraft Show. Annual Goat Show. Senior Inter-County v. Shetland (Football, Hockey & Rugby). Football: Senior Inter-County v. Caithness. Kirkwall Open Golf Championship. Stromness Open Golf Championship.

AUGUST: Agricultural shows (First fortnight): Sanday, East Mainland, Shapinsay, Rousay, St. Margaret's Hope, Dounby and the County Show at Kirkwall. Football: Parish Cup Final at Kirkwall. S & J.D. Robertson Sea Angling Competition. Boys' Ploughing Match and Festival of the Horse: South Ronaldsay. Kirkwall Regatta. St. Magnus Fair: Kirkwall. Wideford Hill Race. Orkney Motorcross Club one-day event. The Riding of the Marches: Kirkwall. Flower Shows. Orkney Vintage Club Rally. Eday Gala Week. Inter-County Athletics: Orkney v. Caithness. Inter-County Football: Orkney v. Shetland on alternate years.

SEPTEMBER: Orkney Open Athletic Championship. Northern Isles Open Boat Festival and Orkney Open Boat Sea Angling Competition. Kirkwall - Stromness Road Relay Race. County Sheepdog Trials. Chrysanthemum & Dahlia Show: Kirkwall.

OCTOBER: 'Ling' Sea Angling Competition. SWRI Baking Show. Exhibition by Orkney Art Students at the Pier Arts Centre, Stromness.

NOVEMBER: Annual Guy Fawkes Bonfire and Fireworks display at Pickaquoy, Kirkwall. Piano Festival & Young Musicians of the Year: Stromness. Harvest Homes. Salvation Army Annual Service of Male Voice Praise in Kirkwall. Orkney Cage Bird Society's Open Show: Kirkwall.

DECEMBER: St. Colm's Centre Christmas Fair: Kirkwall. Christmas Exhibition of work by Orkney artists: Stromness. Fatstock Show and Sale: Kirkwall and Stromness Auction Marts. Annual Pantomime: Kirkwall Arts Club. Christmas Day Ba': Kirkwall. Model Yacht Regatta: Sanday (26 Dec.)

MAINLAND
AND
SOUTH ISLES

Brough of Birsay
Birsay
Eynhallow Sd.
L. Swannay
EVIE
Dounby
Bay of Skaill
Yesnaby
L. of Harray
Finstown
Wide Firth
B. of Firth
Br. of Waith
L. of Stenness
Kirkwall
MAINLAND
Shapinsay Sound
Rerwick Hd.
Mull Hd.
Stromness
Ward Hill 881 ft
ORPHIR
ST. ANDREWS
Deer Sd.
DEERNESS
Pt. of Ayre
Graemsay
HOLM
St. Mary's
Copinsay
Hoy Pier
1565 ft.
Ward Hill
Cava
Scapa Flow
Holm Sd.
Rose Ness
Old Man of Hoy
Rackwick
Rora Hd.
Hoy
Fara
Flotta
Burray
St. Margaret's Hope
Melsetter
Cantick Hd.
South Ronaldsay
Tor Ness
Swona
Burwick
Brough Ness
Pentland Firth
Dunnet Head
Stroma
Pentland Skerries
Gill's Bay
John O' Groats
Duncansby Head
Dunnet
Dunnet Bay.
Caithness

SCALE
0   5   10
MILES

8

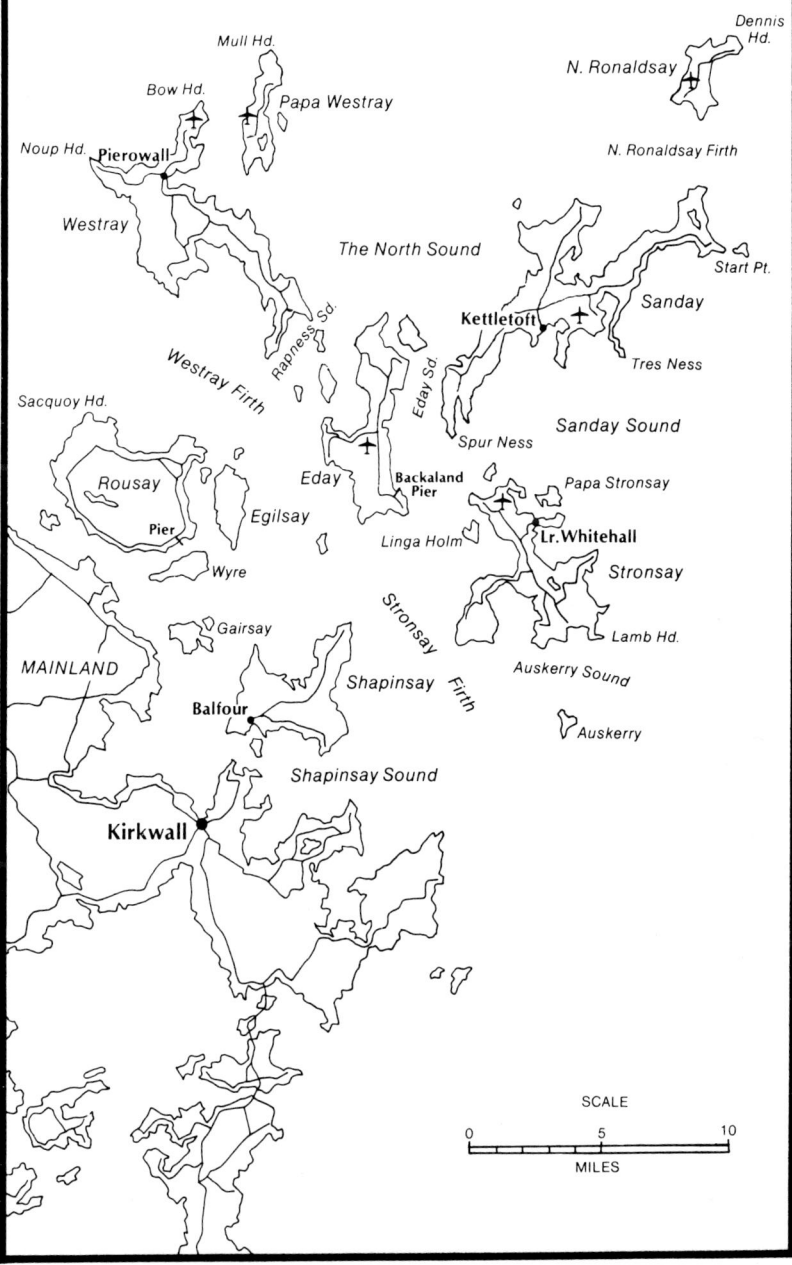

NORTH ISLES

Mull Hd.

Dennis Hd.

N. Ronaldsay

Bow Hd.

Papa Westray

Noup Hd. **Pierowall**

N. Ronaldsay Firth

Westray

The North Sound

Start Pt.

Rapness Sd.

Kettletoft

Sanday

Westray Firth

Eday Sd.

Tres Ness

Sacquoy Hd.

Sanday Sound

Spur Ness

Rousay

Eday

Backaland Pier

Papa Stronsay

Pier

Egilsay

Linga Holm

Lr. Whitehall

Wyre

Stronsay

Gairsay

Stronsay Firth

Lamb Hd.

MAINLAND

Shapinsay

Auskerry Sound

Balfour

Shapinsay Sound

Auskerry

Kirkwall

SCALE

0   5   10

MILES

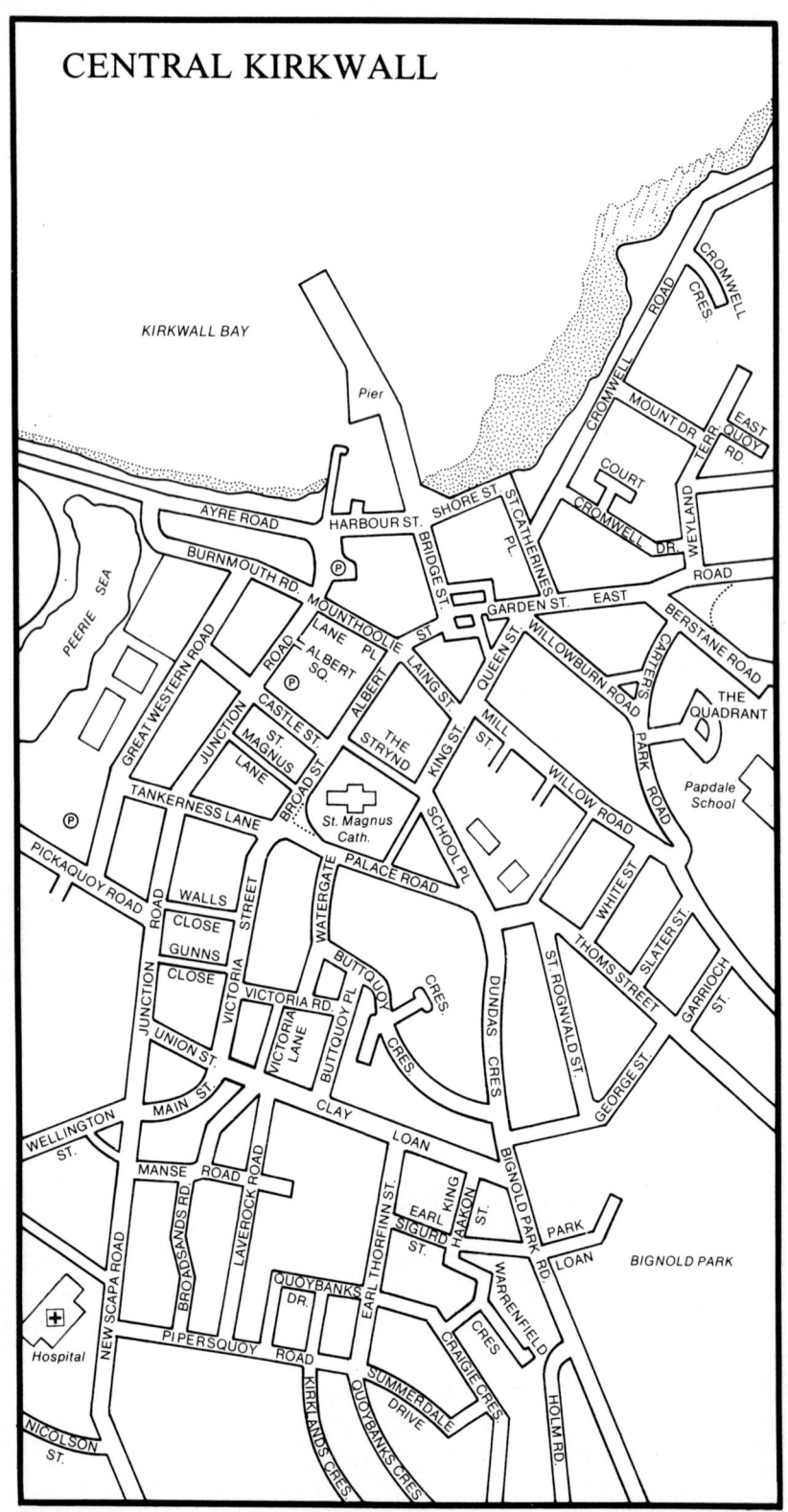

CENTRAL KIRKWALL

KIRKWALL BAY

PEERIE SEA

Pier

AYRE ROAD

BURNMOUTH RD.

HARBOUR ST.

SHORE ST.

BRIDGE ST.

ST. CATHERINES PL.

GARDEN ST.

EAST

CROMWELL

ROAD

CROMWELL

CRES.

MOUNT DR.

EAST QUOY RD.

WEYLAND TERR.

COURT

CROMWELL DR.

ROAD

BERSTANE ROAD

CARTER'S PARK ROAD

THE QUADRANT

Papdale School

GREAT WESTERN ROAD

MOUNTHOOLIE LANE

ROAD

ALBERT PL.

ALBERT SQ.

CASTLE ST.

MAGNUS LANE

JUNCTION ROAD

BROAD ST.

LAING ST.

THE STRYND

KING ST.

QUEEN ST.

WILLOWBURN ROAD

MILL ST.

WILLOW ROAD

WHITE ST.

SLATER ST.

GARRIOCH ST.

TANKERNESS LANE

St. Magnus Cath.

PALACE ROAD

SCHOOL PL.

WATERGATE

PICKAQUOY ROAD

JUNCTION ROAD

WALLS CLOSE

GUNNS CLOSE

VICTORIA STREET

VICTORIA RD.

VICTORIA LANE

BUTTQUOY PL.

BUTTQUOY CRES.

CRES.

DUNDAS CRES.

ST. ROGNVALD ST.

THOMS STREET

GEORGE ST.

UNION ST.

WELLINGTON ST.

MAIN ST.

MANSE ROAD

LAVEROCK ROAD

BROADSANDS RD.

NEW SCAPA ROAD

CLAY

LOAN

QUOYBANKS DR.

PIPERSQUOY ROAD

EARL THORFINN ST.

EARL SIGURD ST.

KING HAAKON ST.

WARRENFIELD CRES.

CRAIGIE CRES.

SUMMERDALE DRIVE

QUOYBANKS CRES.

KIRKLANDS CRES.

BIGNOLD PARK RD.

PARK LOAN

BIGNOLD PARK

HOLM RD.

Hospital

NICOLSON ST.

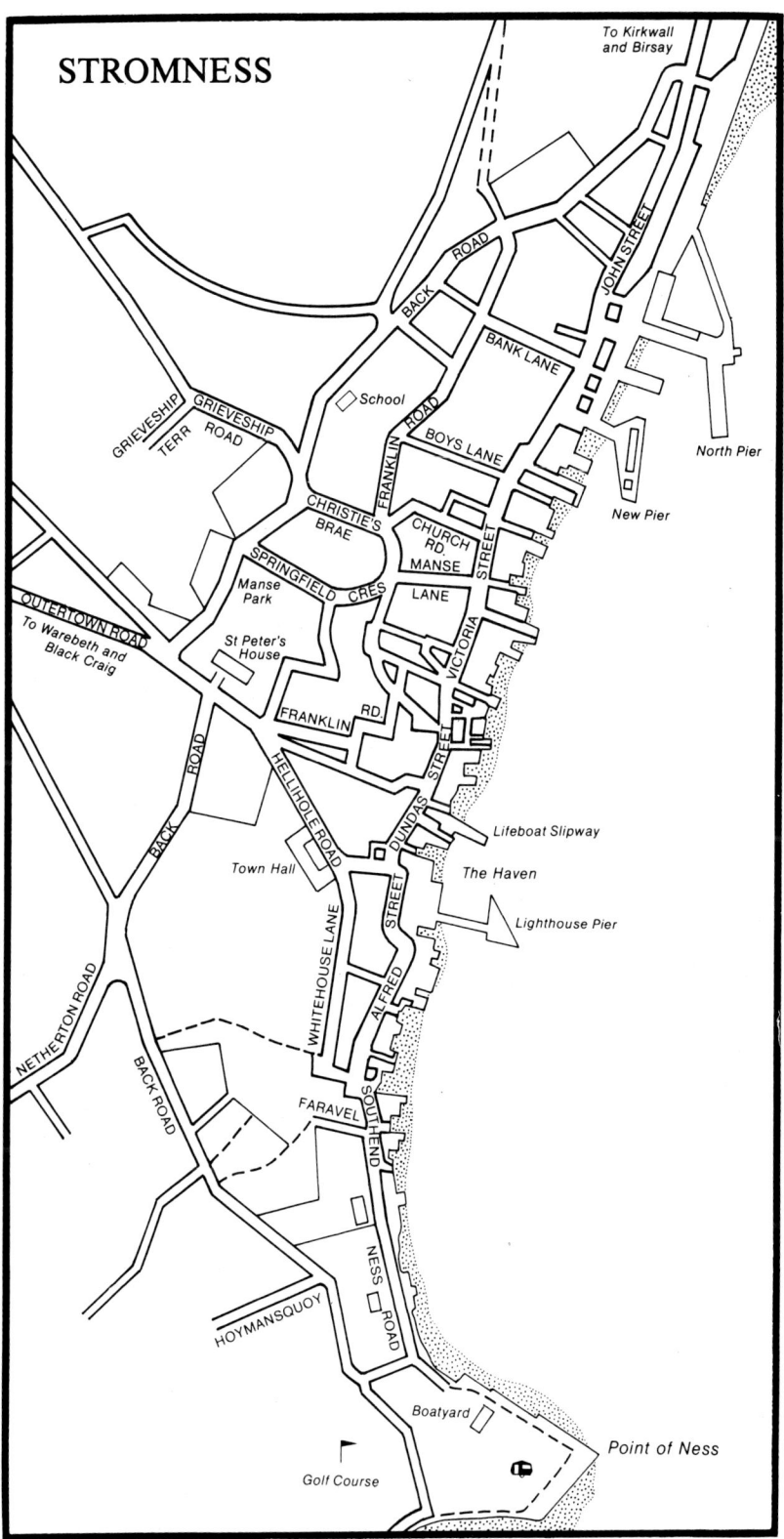

STROMNESS

The Orkney Landscape

Ronald Miller

A visitor to Orkney coming north by road or rail enjoys some 200 miles of magnificent Highland scenery—steep craggy hills, rocky outcrops everywhere and low ground either boggy or underlaid with sand or gravel. Very picturesque, but poverty-stricken. He naturally expects, when he gets to the end of the road, Orkney, to encounter something quite outstandingly wretched. Sailing from Scrabster to Stromness, his fears are confirmed, for in front of him are the barren hills of Hoy. From Rora Head to the Kame he is, unless the Firth is exacting its customary tribute, agape at the monumental red sandstone cliffs, culminating in the perpendicular 1000ft of St. John's Head, twice the height of Beachy Head. The Old Man, too, is as upstanding as any Highland rock-face.

But when he rounds the Kame of Hoy, and for the rest of his sojourn in Orkney, he is in a douce, green fecund countryside with low smoothly-contoured hills and, with the notable exception of the coast, not an outcrop of rock in sight. In one field he can see more cattle than there are in many a Highland parish, but he will be hard put to find small black-faced sheep on heather moorland.

In ancient geological times, when life was just beginning to appear on earth, the site of Orkney was occupied by a vast lake into which sediments were poured over a long period. Conditions, however, oscillated cyclically; coarse sands were followed by finer, by flagstones, shales, clays and fine mudstones which are often virtually limestones. Apart from some faulting, minor folds and tertiary dykes, the sediments have been undisturbed and lie horizontally or only slightly inclined. The floor and shores of the lake, however, consist of Highland rocks, and knobs of these ancient crystalline gneisses and granites protrude in the Stromness area, with outcrops from Graemsay to Yesnaby, showing miniature Highland characteristics, with bare rock, thin acid soils and a heather covering. In the conglomerates flanking the crystalline masses, uranium ore has been concentrated, especially to the immediate north and north-east of Stromness. This is one resource whose exploitation is fiercely resisted by Orcadians, for it would not only sever the land communications of Stromness with the rest of the Mainland but would create widespread radioactive pollution of land, sea and air.

For the most part the sediments were laid down in discrete layers. Sometimes the lake was so shallow that ripple-marks were formed, sometimes desert conditions prevailed, and false-bedded sandstones resulted, as in the Red Head of Eday (or St. Magnus Cathedral). Such conditions prevailed at the end of the period, giving rise to a great thickness of the red sandstones which now form the high ground of Hoy. Commonly, however, the beds are more or less flaggy. Thin beds, an inch or so thick, make convenient roof coverings—the 'gray slates' of old houses. Those two or three inches thick make good paving slabs or, again, roofing material which has the advantage of not requiring sawn timber for its support—an important consideration in wind-swept treeless Orkney. Thicker beds furnish very convenient building stone, with two parallel flat sides, so that almost anyone can be a builder. Probably the finest of this material comes from Walliwell quarry, just outside Kirkwall and most of the better nineteenth century buildings there demonstrate what superlative masonry it can create. Even our earliest ancestors, ill equipped with tools, were able to erect some fine buildings, such as Maeshowe. Indeed, when the Cathedral was built it was the largest and finest in all Scandinavia.

The flaggy nature of most of the bed-rock profoundly influences the character of our exposed coasts and the fact that the beds are sub-horizontal gives the cliffs their commonly vertical form. The sea pounds at the base of the cliff, compressing air far into the bedding planes and joints in the rock. On the recoil, this air expands, creating an outward thrust, so that caves are readily formed and sometimes penetrate far inland and, when the roof collapses, form that distinctive Orkney feature, a 'gloup'. Stacks, of which the Old Man of Hoy is only the largest, are also characteristic of the flagstones, especially where a fault or a dyke has created a line of weakness which the sea can exploit.

But not all the coasts are under attack: in sheltered situations and where the off-shore slope is gentle, material is cast ashore and built, not eroded, forms prevail. Sometimes this consists merely of sand rich in comminuted shells and thus equivalent to a ground limestone which, when blown inland as it often is, produced high fertility and easy tillage for early settlers. In many Orkney parishes the initial settlement and often the parish church is behind a sandy beach. The Island of Sanday, which is essentially a series of islets linked by sandy bars and beaches, is yielding striking evidence of early and dense settlement.

The last phase in the geological evolution of Scotland was a series of glaciations. In periods of maximum, the ice-sheet enveloping Orkney came from across the North Sea, plastering a layer of clay and stones over the land, deeper on low ground and thin or absent on the hills. The heavy terminal morainic boulders, as recent oil-related exploration has revealed, were, happily, dumped on the sea-bed to the westward and Orkney was thus spared the trains of boulders that so characteristically encumber ground that was at an ice margin. Only towards the end of the Ice Age did a small ice-sheet, from the Highlands, terminate in Orkney, leaving the broken belt of small hillocks which extend from Dounby to Finstown and again to the west of St. Mary's, Holm. Only in Hoy was the land high enough to nourish a local glacier at this stage and the corrie and moraine formed by it are there to see in north-west Hoy, between the Enegars and the Kame.

The bed-rock, except where it is a massive sandstone, weathers to form an excellent soil. The glacial clays are also fertile, but often wet, for it was laid down haphazardly, has no organised drainage and may even form dams and consequently lochs. The climate is cool but not very rainy—wetter than Edinburgh but drier than Glasgow—but in winter the isles are swept by gale after gale, which does much to dry the ground, even on the clays. The Hebridean-type blanket bog does not occur in Orkney. In summer, drought is rare and grass remains richly green all season.

But there are, in contrast, dark heather moorlands ('black hill' to Orcadians) which cap some of the higher ground. This moorland is developed on acid peat which was formed about 1000 BC when the climate deteriorated to wet, cold conditions. For early man, black hill must have dominated all but the areas of blown shell-sand and particularly well-drained spots. The inhabitants of the time must have suffered particularly hard conditions and much of their food must have come from the sea. Over the centuries, by dint of turning over the peat and especially by the application of shell sand, the soil was sweetened and fertilised and grass and corn crops took over. It has to be realised, therefore, that much of the fertile farmland to be seen today is not natural but the creation of generations of diligent Orcadians: indeed the process still continues, to the alarm of those who see the moorlands and wetlands as the last refuge of wild life.

If the name of the isles had to be modified, it would be a fitting tribute to the enormous human effort that has created the smiling fertile fields to call them 'The Green Isles of Orkney'.

Archaeology

Raymond Lamb

Man arrived late in Orkney. During the hundreds of thousands of years of the Old Stone Age, Orkney lay under ice; and no indication has been found of habitation by 'hunter-gatherer' communities of the Middle Stone Age, who colonised Scotland as the ice-sheets retreated after about 10,000 BC. In fact, the first colonists—who on present indications did not arrive much before 4000 BC—were Neolithic (New Stone Age) farmers, and farming has remained the most important occupation in Orkney ever since.

The remarkable preservation of prehistoric monuments arises from the scarcity of wood and the abundance of flagstone. Timber-built equivalents of Skara Brae doubtless existed throughout Britain, but in Orkney the flagstone was used instead of wooden posts and beams. The stone furniture in the Skara Brae houses gives an immediate impression of homely life which has made the place justly famous; it dates around 3100-2500 BC. On Papa Westray is a pair of oblong houses which are some 500 years older, and may perhaps be the oldest upstanding houses in Western Europe. In the Knap of Howar houses can still be seen the quernstones on which these earliest farming people ground their grain.

But of the Neolithic period, Orkney shows the visitor more tombs than houses, and it can be confusing to try to relate the two. This is an outstanding archaeological problem, for the Neolithic age lasted some 2000 years, and the pottery types found in tombs and houses do not always match up as one would like. The Skara Brae people had a distinctive pottery called 'grooved ware', some further finds of which have led to suggestions that the inhabitants of this type of settlement used, if they did not actually construct, tombs of the kind named after Maes Howe, which have small side-chambers opening off a central large chamber. Maes Howe itself, an astounding monument, is the finest chambered tomb in Europe; others of the type can be visited at Cuween (near Finstown), Quoyness (Sanday) and Vinquoy Hill (Eday).

Another and numerous type of tomb has a long, narrow chamber divided by upright slabs into compartments like the stalls in a stable or byre. The 'stalled cairn' at Midhowe on the Island of Rousay is very long indeed; more ordinary ones can be seen on the same island at Yarso and Blackhammer and on Mainland at Onstan. Chambered tombs begin in the fourth and extend through the third millennium BC, the Maes-Howe tombs being rather later than the stalled ones; the habitations of the stalled-cairn builders may perhaps have been houses like Knap of Howar, a speculation which is a subject of current research.

Recent excavations at Quanterness (Mainland) and Isbister (South Ronaldsay) have shown how the tombs were used. Each seems to have been the burying-place for the population of a particular area, and the function was that of a charnel-house rather than a grave. Into the chambers were cast the loose bones of corpses from which the flesh had been removed by prolonged exposure in the open. In the later Neolithic period, alongside the tombs, the great ritual monuments began to develop, the great circles of Stenness and Brogar reaching their full perfection at the beginning of the Bronze Age. In the Bronze Age, after 2000 BC, there is a change of style; the collective tombs give way to individual burials, often cremations, involving cists, urns and often a small burial-mound. This is taken to imply a change to a less egalitarian society, but little change is apparent in the style of living or the overall pattern of settlement.

In the late Bronze Age, after 1000 BC, there is increasing evidence of major upheavals. Farming and settlement retreated from the hill lands, the climate

The Ring of Brogar

became cooler and wetter, and peat began to form on what had been reasonable farmland. As we enter the Iron Age, about 600 BC, settlement—which up to now had been evenly scattered—became nucleated, as people took to clustering together in densely built-up little villages which, in response to social disorder, were fortified. Elaborate defences were developed, culminating by the end of the millennium in the tower-like massive structures which archaeologists misleadingly call brochs.

'Broch' in fact is the local derivative of Old Norse *borg* which had the very wide meaning of any strong, defensive or elevated place. The Norsemen applied it freely to all these elaborately-defended settlements which by their time littered the landscape, as well as to promontory forts, rocky islets, and the like (*Brough*, as in the Brough of Birsay, is another spelling of the same word). What the Early Iron Age fortified settlement comprised very often was a more or less tower-like massive central structure—the 'broch' of the archaeologists—surrounded by densely-packed dwellings and enclosed within outer defences. Gurness in the North Mainland is the best example, while at Midhowe in Rousay the tower and dwellings are tightly packed into a promontory fort. The effect is not unlike that of a mediaeval castle with its keep and baileys, and Early Iron Age society very likely was organised on hierarchical lines, possibly having something in common with mediaeval feudalism. These broch-settlements probably continued in habitation well into the first millennium AD; at a time when their peoples emerged into history as the Picts, they probably were still the centres of power when the first Christian missionaries arrived. These came in the eighth century, and were soon followed by colonising Norsemen.

Virtually nothing is known of the process by which Pictish Orkney became Scandinavian. *The Orkneyinga Saga,* which relates the affairs of the Jarls or rulers, is silent on the matter. The language of the Picts at any rate was eliminated, and Orkney's place names are overwhelmingly Norse. In the late eighth and ninth centuries Orkney must have been a base for Viking raids on the monasteries of England and Ireland; but the Norsemen revealed by the archaeological and place-name records were farmers. 'Going a-viking' was a popular and profitable sideline for farmers, or the sons of farmers, during the slack periods between spring sowing and hay-harvest, and between hay-harvest and corn-harvest. There are increasing indications that the progress of Christianity, begun among the Picts in the immediately pre-Norse period, continued through the ninth and tenth centuries, with the incomers adopting the new religion within a generation or two. The saga, however, indicates that the ruling elite—the Jarl and his household—remained pagan down to the death of Sigurd the Stout in 1014.

15

The Orkneyinga Saga vividly conveys the spirit of the age, and Orkney today retains its Norse pattern of settlement. For this reason Norse farmsteads are, as archaeological objects, hard to find, for their sites have continued in occupation to the present day. In mediaeval times, churches did not stand isolated in the countryside, but were built close by important farms; and there are places, such as the old Cross Kirks in Sanday and Westray, where a now isolated church-ruin marks the location of a vanished farmstead, the remains of which can be detected by the observant. Kirkwall began as a Norse trading-centre and contains the most spectacular monument of the Jarldom, the twelfth-century St. Magnus Cathedral built by the best masons of the time, testifying to the wealth and prestige of Orkney in its Norse 'golden age'.

Coming right up to date, Orkney has probably the best assemblage of monuments relating to the defence of Britain in 1914-18 and 1939-45, notably the shore batteries which held heavy naval guns. The relics are numerous, on the whole they are not beautiful but they are historically evocative and military enthusiasts will find enough material to fill a holiday. In Scapa Flow, the sorry remnant of von Tirpitz's High Seas Fleet now attracts many visitors whose archaeological enthusiasm has extended under water.

The archaeologically-minded visitor can occupy a full week in seeing the well-publicised monuments in official guardianship on the Mainland and on the adjacent and easily-reached Island of Rousay. The bigger monuments have individual 'Official Guides', and all are covered in the HMSO booklet *Ancient Monuments of Orkney* by Anna and Graham Ritchie. The spectacular archaeological potential of the outer islands remains largely unexploited, and every visitor should now take advantage of improving transport services to visit two or three of these. Information on the archaeological sites, not otherwise well known, is given in a series of island guide leaflets which can be picked up gratis at the Tourist Office and other places. Westray is worth visiting for Noltland Castle, Papa Westray for Knap of Howar and chambered tombs on its adjacent Holm. The Heritage Walk in Eday (day package trip from Kirkwall available in season) takes in prehistoric tombs, a standing stone, enclosures and field boundaries.

Sanday has most to offer the serious archaeologist, while Hoy has military interest; a visitors' centre is now open in the old Lyness dockyard.

St. Magnus Cathedral

Kirkwall

Marjorie Linklater

Kirkwall, the capital town of the Orkney Islands, has been the commercial and administrative centre since the eleventh century. Its name is from the Norse *Kirkjuvagr* (Church Bay) after the church built by Earl Rognvald Bruisison around the year 1040 in memory of his friend King Olaf Harraldsson later the patron saint of Norway. Nothing remains of this church except the doorway in St. Olaf's Wynd—one of the many wynds and closes so characteristic of this ancient burgh.

The *Kirk*, or church, therefore existed long before the Cathedral of St. Magnus whose splendour dominates the town and has done for over 800 years. Earl Rognvald Kolsson (to distinguish him from the builder of the older church) built the cathedral, dedicated to his martyred uncle, Magnus, in 1137.

The Cathedral is the centre of the town, or city, indeed the centre of the whole archipelago—the Orcades. Opposite its south door, across the road, is the imposing ruin of the Bishop's Palace, part of it founded in the twelfth century and rebuilt in the sixteenth century by Bishop Reid. After the battle of Largs in 1263 King Haakon came back to Orkney and died in the Bishop's Palace.

The Earl's Palace further up the road was built by Earl Patrick Stewart of infamous memory. It has been called the finest structure of the sixteenth century in Scotland.

Northwards you may find a plaque in the wall of the Aberdeen Savings Bank, Castle Street, marking the site of Kirkwall Castle. Earl Henry St. Clair of Caithness built this stronghold on the edge of the sea, which at that time covered the land up to what is now Junction Road. The Castle, built in 1382, was described in contemporary records as the Earl's 'little court in Orkney the most elegant and refined in Europe.'

The burgh and city of Kirkwall received a Royal Charter from James III on 31 March 1486: 'To erect all & haill our said Burgh and City of Kirkwall and the part called Laverock, in ane full Burgh Royal.' Laverock, southwards, was the Bishop's domain, while in the direction of Kirkwall Castle secular authority ruled.

That is why, annually on Christmas Day and New Year's Day the ancient rivalry between *Crown and Mitre* is re-enacted when men of Kirkwall gather for The Ba'. 'Uppies and Doonies' they are called nowadays, taking political steam out of the conflict. But plenty of steam is generated as the two sides confront each other in the struggle to reach the goal at either end of the city with the Ba'. To the uninitiated, rules and tactics appear to be totally absent, but in fact the contest is directed from the heart of the scrum by leaders who know when to heave, when to break, when to 'smuggle'. So the bystander has to be wary. That mass of humanity locked immobile (sometimes up to half an hour in one place) at the mouth of the close or wynd, will suddenly break and a torrent of yelling savages—as many as two hundred at times—will burst in pursuit of the man with the ball, a mighty wave threatening to engulf spectators careless enough to linger at the other end of the lane. The Men's Ba' on Christmas Day 1982 lasted seven hours from 'throw-up' on Kirk Green in front of the Cathedral to 'splash-down' in the Harbour.

The Harbour is a good starting point for exploration. Here the boats which serve the North Isles are berthed, and the basin is crowded with craft of every kind. On summer evenings sailing-boats compete in Points races which culminate in the Regatta on a Saturday in August. Boats can be hired here for sea-angling and at Scapa. Orkney Tourist Organisation in Broad Street supplies information about this and other recreations.

Kirkwall Harbour

The earliest settlement clustered round Shore Street where, until recently old houses existed on the site where now there are unsightly oil-tanks. In fact, a little further on, the offices of today's oil-distributors stand where once whales from Greenland and 'caain' whales driven ashore on the islands, were boiled to provide oil for Orkney's *cruisie* lamps. Dunkirk Lane leading to Cromwell Road gets its name from Earl Patrick Stewart's finest ship which sailed in these waters in the 1590s. And Cromwell's soldiers built a Fort on the headland eastwards to guard the entrance to the harbour.

Returning to the pier-head overlooked by the Kirkwall Hotel, turn into Bridge Street, the beginning of the town's long paved thoroughfare where modern shops occupy charming old buildings. There are many good restaurants in Kirkwall which it would be invidious to mention separately, except for the Ship Inn which is the same Ship Inn where Sir Walter Scott dined in 1814 and wrote disparaging verses about Kirkwall, having had to pay for the meal owing to the parsimony of the City Fathers. It is next to a fish shop (by Royal Charter) which was originally the town house of Provost Craigie of Gairsay, built by him in the seventeenth century. On the opposite side of the street a Victorian emporium and solid warehouses have been adapted to modern commerce. In fact you can find just about anything here.

Bridge Street becomes Albert Street as it turns right. Town houses of the country lairds can be identified by archways and paved courtyards. Here and there stone lintels with coats of arms and initials denote the residences of worthies notable in their time and recorded in the archives of the Library to be found in Laing Street (left, halfway along Albert Street), the oldest Public Library in Scotland, founded in 1683.

The Big Tree which once grew to a fair height in the centre of the roadway in Albert St., became unsafe, and was pollarded (truncated) in 1987. Returning to Broad St., the Strynd—a lane on your left—is worth looking at. The row of houses, the oldest in the town, have been restored for public use, and the lane emerges opposite the Orkney Islands Council offices, once the Kirkwall Grammar School. The new school is on the perimeter of the town, purpose-built and during the holidays provides the community with a swimming pool and sports centre.

Kirkwall can boast an excellent little Theatre in Mill Street. Amateur Drama and Opera are enormously popular. So are travelling performances sponsored by the Scottish Arts Council and a variety of other entertainment.

Back to Broad Street where you will find Tankerness House Museum. Above the archway the carved lintel shows the date 1574 along with the coat of arms of Gilbert Foulzie, the last Catholic Archdeacon and first Protestant priest in Kirkwall—symbolic of Orkney's tolerance, ecclesiastical and political. The Town Hall, built in 1884 is now a Community Centre; aggressively Victorian amid the graceful architecture of earlier periods, it is old enough now to be venerated and admired.

Victoria Street is a continuation of the main thoroughfare and, as this was church property, it is where the affluent citizens lived. The Royal Hotel occupies two houses, one facing squarely on to the street and the adjacent house gable-ended to the street and overlooking a courtyard. A carved lintel above what was once the front door is dated 1670. Above the street-facing door is the date 1679. Maybe social habits were changing and privacy was giving way to the entertainment offered by watching the comings and goings on the street. By the nineteenth century the well-to-do were removing themselves from the congested area of commerce and building solid houses up Palace Road. Even the Paterson Church (now called the East Church) is above the Cathedral, and the Episcopal Church of St. Olaf is further up still, claiming prestige from its connection with the Kirk by the Bay.

Back at the lower level, Victoria Street crosses Clay Loan and becomes Main Street. The fine facade of the West End Hotel is unchanged from the time when this was the town house of the Balfours of Shapinsay. And for those who are tired of history and architecture there is the popular Pavilion opposite. Once there were tennis courts here, now snooker is the fashion and electronic games.

The street ends at the intersection of Junction Road which becomes New Scapa Road. The Catholic Church is on the corner.

Scapa Beach is only a mile from this end of Kirkwall, with the Orkney Harbour Authority H.Q. and the pier that serves Flotta and the south end of Hoy. There is an enjoyable walk from Scapa to Inganess Bay and back to Kirkwall, a distance of approximately four miles. The path crosses farmland and two main roads. There are stiles and sign-posts saying 'Bridle-path'. This walk is perhaps better approached from the Holm Road taking the walker through the precincts of the Highland Park Distillery. Westward from Scapa Beach is a delightful cliff-top walk with views of the South Isles and a variety of birds and wild-flowers in season.

Finally, golfers can enjoy the eighteen-hole course half a mile outside the town on the Stromness Road.

There are at least six hotels plus B&B accommodation, a Youth Hostel and Caravan Park. Many excellent shops sell knitwear, Orkney-designed jewellery, pottery and leatherwork. Other specialities are farm cheeses, shortbread and biscuits from Westray where Orkney chairs are also made. Fish, shell-fish and Orkney beef are of prime quality and there is a line in home-made pâtés and flans. Indeed local bakers carry on a tradition of high quality. There are the usual supermarkets and take-away caterers. Early closing is Wednesday.

Sunset over Maes Howe

Stromness

George Mackay Brown

Stromness looks much older, more 'sunk in time' than its neighbour Kirkwall; but in fact it is quite a modern town.

Visitors are at once impressed by a quality of uniqueness—the hill Brinkie's Brae behind, the secure harbour in front, the single street that meanders and dips and surges along the eastern margin of the voe.

The houses, it seems, were thrown up at random, without any plan or aesthetic consideration, mostly in the eighteenth century. The main street is beautiful and full of surprises; but the street is only one of the delights Stromness has to offer. From the street without pavements closes radiate, reaching towards the granite of Brinkie's Brae, stepping down to the piers of fishermen, with creels and boats and cormorants and gulls.

Nowadays Stromness, with its 1700 people, is a quiet place. There is a little stir when the ferry-boat *St. Ola* comes in from Scrabster in Scotland in the early afternoon. Fishing boats, with flocks of attendant gulls, come into the harbour from the Atlantic storms. On a Wednesday the farmers and their wives drive in to the mart and the shops.

One week in late July is given over to high revelry—it is Stromness's summer festival, now well established since its start in 1949.

There is a Sunday in midsummer when Stromness is the centre of the five-day-long St. Magnus Festival; then famous musicians perform in the Academy Hall, and Peter Maxwell Davies gives one of his brilliant talks on music in the Pier Arts Centre.

The Pier Arts Centre: this beautiful complex, recently restored on an old mercantile pier, has a permanent collection of works of the St Ives school (Barbara Hepworth, Ben Nicholson, etc.) and also changing exhibitions by other artists, many of them local. It is a pleasant place to wander through, with the sea glitter on the walls. Also poetry sounds wonderful, read in it.

Fascinating too, and established for many generations, is the Museum at the South End. There too, year after year, are changing exhibitions designed with artistry and imagination.

Stromness and the hills of Hoy

Stromness was not always such a quiet place, except perhaps in its medieval beginnings, when there was a small monastery near where the present kirkyard is, and a Norse castle at Cairston on the far side of the voe. We can imagine—though there is no record of it—a hamlet of fishermen's huts under Brinkie's Brae. (It is one of the safest havens in Orkney, with rich fishing grounds off Hoy and Yesnaby.). A sixteenth century bishop built his fine house three miles to the north-west.

Suddenly a written record: a man called William Clark wants to build an inn, in late sixteenth century, right at the tip of the voe. Larger merchant ships were beginning to seek sanctuary from Atlantic storms, possibly *en route* between Europe and America. Orkneymen with a few guineas in a chest under the bed saw 'with a wild surmise' that they could cash in on this trade, buying and selling, getting and spending; even building their own ships and trading to Scandinavia and the Baltic. It was then, probably, that the town we recognise as Stromness came into being in the matter of a few decades. Dwelling-houses and warehouses for merchants were built on a dozen or more stone piers projecting above the harbour water. Then, there must have been a great stir along the unpaved street and on the waterfronts.

And that activity was but the beginning, for the Hudson's Bay Company ships called annually at Stromness for replenishment and to recruit young Orkneymen for the fur-stations in Canada. Whaling ships called, on their way to and from Greenland; and twice a year the whaling men held wild revelry in the town, whereby the sober townsfolk were sore affronted.

Stromness must have been a fascinating place to live in during the eighteenth century, with such larger-than-life people as Alexander Graham, Gow the Pirate, Bessie Millie the seller of winds.

The modern town, though of course it has large accretions of council houses, must be recognisably the same as it was 200 years ago.

But the boisterous music of the opening movement has changed—it is now a quiet andante, with summer stirrings of tourists and festival. What the next movement will be we cannot guess. We can only hope that the symphony, when it is complete, will have a good shape to it.

Around the Mainland

Howie Firth

Orkney's west coast offers a variety of beach and cliff walks, from Stromness at the southern end to Birsay in the north. Stromness Community Council, in fact, have printed a leaflet on walks in the south-west mainland, and it is available in French, German, Norwegian and Italian, as well as English. The cliff-top walk between Stromness and Yesnaby provides views of bird-colonies and breaking sea, though care is needed near all Orkney cliffs. Yesnaby, a quarter-hour's drive from Stromness, has some bleak remains of wartime structures, but the Bay of Skaill, further north, has a beautiful sandy beach, and the Stone Age village of Skara Brae.

The next turning off towards the sea leads to the township of Marwick, and a parking-space from which a short walk takes you to the cliff-top of Marwick Head. Green grass gives way to the sudden sight of the sea beating on the rocks below, and fulmars soaring past on the updraughts. Panoramic views of land and sea open out around you, but just as striking is the nearby tower of the Kitchener Memorial, that marks the events of the stormy night of 5 June 1916, when the British cruiser *Hampshire* with the Secretary of State for War

Skara Brae

aboard struck a German mine off Marwick Head and sank. Only twelve men survived.

Further north, there are attractive rocky shores at Birsay, with the road northwards giving an open view of the village known as 'The Palace', before taking an apparent wide detour to take you there. The view of Birsay also shows the tidal island known as the Brough, and the road to Birsay passes Boardhouse Mill, the only working meal mill left in Orkney.

The road beyond the Palace to the Brough of Birsay ends in a parking space, and then, keeping a careful eye on the tide, you may be able to walk across the causeway to the Brough, or else follow the coastline from the Point of Buckquoy on past various inlets and skerries with fascinating names – Skippi Geo, Lynaber, Doonaminya and Longaber.

The drive round the north coast from Birsay, through Swannay to Evie, gives fine views of Rousay and the little island of Eynhallow between it and the Orkney mainland. Behind Rousay can be seen the cliffs of Westray, and then Egilsay and the tower of St. Magnus Church come into view. Tingwall Jetty is the departure point for a trip to Rousay, Egilsay or Wyre, the island where the poet Edwin Muir spent his boyhood; while the ruined broch of Gurness is nearby.

A long straight road goes on to Finstown, but there are several little hill roads that make a pleasant alternative to explore. Finstown itself takes its name from David Phin, an Irishman who fought at Waterloo, and set up in Finstown a hostelry called the Toddy Hole (today the Pomona Inn). It lies on the Bay of Firth, once famous for oysters, with a range of low hills behind the village, and Binscarth Woods just outside, by the road to Stromness. The main road to Kirkwall, in the other direction, follows the sea, while the old road to Kirkwall cuts over the land, past on the right-hand side the hill of Keelylang with its television transmitter, and then, on the left, Wideford Hill with several other radio masts.

There are several other ways of leaving Finstown, either going up the Hill of Heddle road to the hills behind the village, or taking the Stromness road for a mile or so past Binscarth, and then turning right into Harray, the only parish in Orkney which does not touch the sea. Harray's hill walks provide a rich compensation, however. The second valley north of Binscarth, Syradale, can be reached by a track from the road at Refuge Corner, and the walk past the upper end of Wasdale Loch leads to a burn that flows along the valley floor, and a series of waterfalls on the hillside.

Another burn can be reached by going on through Harray to the village of Dounby, and then turning right at the cross-roads on the way to Evie. A little way along, an old peat road branches off at the bend, and leads to deep heather, and the sheltered course of the Burn of Rush. The area is known as 'Kit Huntlin's', allegedly after an old lady who was said to have brewed illicit liquor, although the name may in fact have a much older origin.

Dounby is another centre which offers a choice of roads – apart from the right turn to Evie, you can go straight on to Birsay, or turn left to head towards Sandwick or Stromness. Going in this direction, and turning left again at two further cross-roads, the road leads towards Stenness, passing the Ring of Brogar and the Standing Stones.

Reaching the main Kirkwall – Stromness road, there is the option of a left turn in the Kirkwall direction, to pass the chambered cairn of Maes Howe; or of crossing to the Bigswell Road, and the trees and flowers by the burn in 'Happy Valley'; or else, turning right to the village of Stenness. The road to Stromness runs through the village and on to the Brig o' Waith, where the sea on the left meets the Loch of Stenness on the right. Just before the Brig is a turning to the left to Orphir, and just before that is a turning to the right to the chambered cairn at Onston.

The Orphir road can also be reached by taking a left turn at the village of Stenness itself, and then going up over the hill and down into the Bay of Ireland. Despite its appearance, the name is in fact of Norse origin, a point brought out by the spelling on the sign at the Mill of Eyrland, now converted into a private house. The mill stands by the main Orphir road, which runs on to divide into a left-hand fork over Scorra Dale, and a right-hand loop round the sea, to Houton and a view of the wartime anchorage of Scapa Flow. Houton is now the base for the roll-on / roll-off links to the South Isles of Hoy and Flotta. The ferry crosses to Lyness at the southern end of Hoy, although for walkers, a direct motor-boat service to the north end of the island is operated from Stromness.

The road through Orphir to Kirkwall passes Waulkmill Bay, with long flat sands, just beyond an area of low heather-topped cliffs. Kirkwall itself is another central point to start a journey, whether by road, or out by sea to the North Isles, or on the shorter half-hour boat journey to the island of Shapinsay. A mile or so to the south of Kirkwall lies Scapa Beach, with the Harbour Offices near the pier, and the Scapa Distillery at the other end of the bay. Orkney's other distillery, the Highland Park, is passed on another road out of Kirkwall, the south-eastward route to Holm and the Churchill Barriers.

The direct route east from Kirkwall goes past the airport, to St. Andrews and then Deerness. There is a turning down left to Inganess Bay, which makes a pleasant walk, or else, just after reaching the top of the hill overlooking the airport, a right turn goes past 'Catty Maggie's' Quarry, and round back to Kirkwall again.

St. Andrews and Holm can be visited together as part of a circular tour that can include a turning off to see the antiques collection at Graemeshall in Holm. The road east from St. Andrews runs on to the peninsular parish of Deerness, crossing there between St. Peter's Pool on the left, and Dingys-howe on the right. Dingyshowe can be a starting-point for walks along the cliffs, or the road can be followed to its ending by the church at Sandside Bay. The track to the left goes to the Gloup, a deep hole in the ground formed by an old collapse of the roof of a sea cave. The sides are steep, with birds nesting on narrow ledges. Just beyond the Gloup is a stile and a strong path, leading to the Brough of Deerness, a tidal island with a narrow path climbing up to it.

Apart from the main roads, there are many attractive side roads, as well as numerous other places of interest, including craft shops and workshops and restaurants to provide a good Orkney tea at the end of a day's outing.

The North and South Isles

Christine Muir

NORTH RONALDSAY

This island, furthest north of the Orkney archipelago, is one of the most fascinating. By sea and air, the first sight of North Ronaldsay is of a low, green island edged by white sand, and the clear blue water of Nouster Bay. Usually there is a colony of grey seals basking on the beach, and some of the island's most unusual assets, the native sheep, browsing on fresh seaweed thrown up by the tide.

North Ronaldsay is unique in being completely surrounded by a drystone dyke, five to six feet high. This ancient wall serves the purpose of keeping the sheep out on the shores and grassy links, where their seaweed diet is continually renewed by each high tide. Their wool is extremely soft and fine, and varied in colour. The sheep are one of the few remaining examples of community agriculture, and their management is controlled by the Sheep Court, elected every three years.

Many of the houses are built on the longhouse plan, and have heavy flagstone roofs. Some of the older crofts still have a kiln, and a horse mill, relics of an older way of life. North Ronaldsay is intensively cultivated, and highly mechanised. Its fertile soil produces good grass, hay and silage, and beef cattle are the main source of income. Oats, a little bere corn, potatoes and turnips are also grown.

The island is a most important migration centre for many different species of birds, rivalling Fair Isle. In spring it provides nesting sites on shores and marshes, as well as inland. Wild flowers grow in profusion in summer, sheets of golden marsh marigolds, yellow flag iris, lady's smock and marsh orchids, as well as the delicate green-veined grass of Parnassus, round the lochs, and blue lesser bugloss, forget-me-nots, violets, poppies, campion, and many others along the field paths.

North Ronaldsay is famous—or infamous—for the shipwreck of countless ships, which struck the dangerous reefs and skerries around the island. The most dramatic was the wreck of the *Svecia of Gothenburg*, a Swedish East India Company merchantman, heavily armed and carrying a valuable cargo, in 1740. Orkney's first lighthouse was lit here in 1789, and in 1854 the second highest land-based lighthouse in Britain was completed. Its white bands and flashing beam are a vital landmark for ships on the busy North Atlantic route. From the balcony at the top, a superb view of the islands is the reward for having climbed 119 steps.

The island occurs frequently in *The Orkneyinga Saga*. Torv Einar murdered Halfdan Longshanks on the north shore, and claimed his right to Orkney. North Ronaldsay was inhabited long before the Viking period. The Broch of Burrian was the site of interesting archaeological discoveries, including an ox-bone with both Pictish and Christian symbols, a stone with an incised Celtic cross, and an iron sanctus bell. A standing stone with a round hole in it was important in local tradition, and as late as 1700 the islanders danced round the stone at the New Year.

There is a resident doctor, a primary school, a bird observatory and a well-equipped community centre on North Ronaldsay.

Access: By air twice daily, Mon. – Sat. Timetable available from: Loganair Ltd., Kirkwall Airport. Tel. (0856) 2494.
By sea once a week from Kirkwall, according to schedule.
Orkney Islands Shipping Co. Ltd., Kirkwall. Tel. (0856) 2044.

WESTRAY

The largest of the North Isles, Westray has both rich and fertile farmland, and hills with good peat. The west coast is steep, although not rising much above two hundred feet, with spectacular views. Noup Head has marvellous overhanging cliffs of red sandstone, with thousands of seabirds circling above the waves and nesting on the ledges.

Among the many caves below the cliffs is the Gentlemen's Cave in which one of the Orkney Jacobites, a Balfour of Trenabie, found refuge with his friends for a whole winter. Westray Jacobites continued to drink the health of 'the King over the water' in this cave, thus escaping the attention of government spies.

To the east, the land is low-lying. There are beautiful sandy beaches in the bays of Brough, Swartmill and Tuquoy, and three small well-stocked lochs. Most of the island's population is distributed over the lowland area. There are good panoramic views from the top of Fitty Hill, 557 ft., in the south west.

The most impressive sight in Westray is Noltland Castle, built for Gilbert Balfour in 1560. The inhabitants of Westray must have worked for many long hard years to build this z-shaped keep, 87ft. long by 37ft. wide, with square towers at the south-west and north-east corners. The ground floor, entered through the south-west tower, contains the kitchens and store-rooms. What must have been a magnificent wide stairway of a later date leads to the great hall. Gilbert Balfour, with his brothers, was implicated in the murder of Cardinal Beaton at St. Andrews, and later of Lord Darnley. He was finally hanged for treason against the King of Sweden in 1576.

From the castle tower there is a view over north Westray to the harbour of Pierowall, once the second most important Viking base in Orkney, and where many graves were found in the sandy banks. Several had their horses buried with them, and one had a dog. Two were buried in small boats with their weapons, and one had a sword at his side forged in Norway in the eighth century.

Nearby is a ruined medieval church, and a store from the glorious days of the herring fisheries. In the latter half of the nineteenth, and well into the twentieth century, there was intense activity in many Orkney islands. Herring was prolific, and fishing boats came from all over Britain to share in the catches. A more recent development is the modern fish factory at Gill Pier, which was set up in 1968. Crabs and lobsters are processed at the factory, and to increase productivity and to protect it from variable prices and seasons, production includes hamburgers, and chips, as well as white fish.

Westray Knitters Society Ltd, East Surriegarth, Tel Westray 323, produce new designs and traditional patterns. Straw-backed Orkney chairs are made on the island, enquiries to Westray 323. There is a resident doctor, a primary and a junior secondary school. Near Pierowall is a nine-hole golf course, and there is a hotel.

Access: By air from Kirkwall, up to four flights daily, Mon. – Sat.
Loganair Ltd., Kirkwall Airport. Tel. (0856) 2494.
By sea from Kirkwall thrice weekly.
Orkney Islands Shipping Co. Ltd., Kirkwall. Tel. (0856) 2044.

PAPA WESTRAY

This small island, a mile wide and four miles long, lies one mile east of Aikerness in Westray, across Papa Sound. It is one of the most northerly isles, attractive and extremely fertile, and it is still intensively cultivated. Green and low-lying, it has been inhabited since at least 3500 BC.

At the Knap of Howar the oldest standing house in Western Europe was found, an archaeological discovery of great importance. There are two adjacent houses, both of which have been excavated to show hearth and quern, stone shelves and dressers. Artifacts too have been found, which link the people who lived there with the builders of the chambered tombs. On the Holm of Papa Westray there is a large chambered cairn, a hundred feet long, with fourteen cells in the centre chamber passage.

On the eastern shore of Loch Tredwell are the ruins of a chapel dedicated to the Celtic Saint Triduana, who plucked out her beautiful eyes and sent them to King Nechtan the Pict, who had admired them. At one time the chapel was a place of pilgrimage for those suffering from eye troubles. Another Celtic site is that of St. Boniface, where the graveyard contains a hogbacked red sandstone gravestone, and where Celtic crosses carved on stone were found.

In the middle of the island is the old mansion of Holland House, the home of the Traills, former owners of Papa Westray. It was on the farm of Holland that the Knap of Howar was discovered.

Papa Westray is also interesting to ornithologists, for the northern end is now an R.S.P.B. reserve, with a summer warden. North Hill is the nesting site for the largest breeding British colony of Arctic Terns, and there are enormous colonies of kittiwakes and guillemots. On the cliffs of Fowl's Craig there are many species of breeding birds. This is the former home of the Great Auk, the last male being sadly shot here in 1813. It is stuffed and displayed in the British Museum. Water fowl abound at Tredwell Loch, among the marshes and flag irises.

Vegetation too is of special scientific interest, especially at the northern end, where plants common only to old red sandstone grow.

Papa Westray, known locally as Papay (O.N. *Papey*, isle of the priests), has a thriving community co-operative, Tel 08574 267, which provides shopping facilities, as well as accommodation for visitors and has revitalised the island. There is a resident nurse, and a primary school.

Access: The island is mentioned in *The Guinness Book of Records* for the shortest scheduled flight in the world, operating between Westray and Papa Westray, a distance of one and a half miles in two minutes.
By air twice daily from Kirkwall, via Westray, Mon. – Sat.
Loganair Ltd., Kirkwall Airport. Tel. (0856) 2494.
By sea thrice weekly from Kirkwall.
Orkney Islands Shipping Co. Ltd., Kirkwall. Tel. (0856) 2044.

Eynhallow, Rousay and Westray from Burgar Hill

28

OLA GORIE
Original Orkney Jewellery

Innovative modern and traditional designs in beautiful ranges of 9ct. gold and sterling silver jewellery. Every piece of Ola Gorie jewellery whether it be new or a trusted old favourite, meets our exacting standards — reassuring in this age of compromise.
See the full range along with a fantastic selection of cards and gifts at our retail outlet,

THE LONGSHIP
opposite St. Magnus Cathedral,
7-9 Broad Street, Kirkwall, Orkney.
Tel. (0856) 3251.

LYNESS NAVAL BASE, NAVAL CEMETERY
AND INTERPRETATION CENTRE, HOY.

Lyness, Hoy, during two world wars, served the North Atlantic Home
Fleet as a service base. From the natural harbour of Scapa Flow,
Dreadnoughts sailed forth to the Battle of Jutland and to sink the
Bismark, but in 1957, Lyness Base was closed. The pumphouse of
the fuel depot at Lyness now houses photographic and audio visual
displays which interpret the history of the Lyness Base (HMS
Prosperine) and of Scapa Flow during these conflicts. A mock
NAAFI canteen has been established and there are numerous
artefacts on display with historical links with Scapa Flow's naval
heritage. Close by is the naval cemetery which has associations with
some of the most famous incidents in modern naval history.

THE PIER ARTS CENTRE

Stromness   Orkney
(0856) 850209

Permanent Collection of Twentieth Century Painting and Sculpture
Also a Changing Programme of Temporary Exhibitions
Children's Room — Art Library — Poetry Readings
Lectures — Open All Year — Admission Free

Figure in Sycamore   Barbara Hepworth 1931

BALFOUR CASTLE
on the Island of Shapinsay
Boat trips Sundays & Wednesdays.

A tour of Balfour Castle and a walk through the Victorian walled gardens. Tea is served in the castle servants' hall with everything home produced and home baked.

For information on accommodation in the castle please write or Telephone (0856) 71 282.

W. J. STOVE & CO.

COACH, MINI-BUS
AND
CAR HIRERS

GRIND
DEERNESS
Tel. Deerness 215

34

If it's service you want... come and bank with us.

BANK OF SCOTLAND
A FRIEND FOR LIFE

SANDAY

Sanday is one of the largest of the North Isles, approximately sixteen miles long, and shaped rather like a lobster. Its name is well deserved, for its beautiful wide sandy beaches, perpetually increasing, are its most notable feature. Whitemill Bay, Sandquoy, and Lopness must be among the most spectacular in Britain, although they are quiet and tranquil, disturbed only by the cry of the birds which nest in the dunes. A variety of wild flowers grow in the many different habitats of the island.

One of Orkney's greatest chambered cairns, Quoyness, on the tidal island of Elsness, can be visited, and there are numerous other archaeological remains. Barrows, cists, burnt mounds, and Viking burials, as well as broch sites, are part of Sanday's rich past.

More ships were wrecked on Sanday's shores, difficult to see in haze or fog, than on any other Orkney island, with the exception of North Ronaldsay. The Sanday lighthouse, automatic since 1962, is one of Britain's oldest. The tower was erected between 1802-1806, and the original residential buildings are intact. Start Point can be reached on foot at low tide across the sand. In the time of the herring fleets, at the turn of the century, there was a salting and packing house at the village of Kettletoft, named after the Viking Kettil. Now the lobster boats lie out from the pier, or at Otterswick, where they have a well-sheltered anchorage.

Most of the island is intensely cultivated, and high quality beef cattle are reared, thriving on Sanday's rich pasture. An electronics firm, employing local people, exports its products all over the world, and they enjoy a high reputation for their quality. The co-operative, Isle of Sanday Knitters, Ltd, employ about 125 women in Sanday, Eday, North Ronaldsay and Stronsay, to knit fashion garments. Over the last few years the volume of work has greatly increased, and the firm is an important part of the island's economy. Visits can be arranged to the Wool Hall, where wool and garments are packed and despatched by appointment with Mrs. Sinclair, of Lady Post Office.

There is a hotel and a guesthouse at Kettletoft, four shops, a primary and a junior secondary school. A doctor, and a district nurse live on the island, and the vet for Sanday and the other North Isles is also resident here. On the dunes of Plain of Fidge there is a nine-hole golf course, and golf clubs are available from Newark Farm. There are good sea fishing waters round the island.

Access: By air up to four flights daily, Mon. – Sat.
Loganair Ltd., Kirkwall Airport. Tel. (0856) 2494.
By sea thrice weekly from Kirkwall.
Orkney Islands Shipping Co. Ltd., Kirkwall. Tel. (0856) 2044.

EDAY

South-west of Sanday lies Eday, eight miles long, with six attendant holms. It rises dark and spectacular out of the sea, with massive cliffs of red sandstone, including the spectacular Red Head, 200ft. high, overlooking Calf Sound and the Calf of Eday. In this fast-flowing sound, John Gow the pirate was captured and later hanged in 1725. Sailing between the Red Head and the Grey Head on the way to Westray or North Ronaldsay is an unforgettable experience, the air filled with the wheeling of thousands of seabirds.

Bird watchers can find much to interest them on Eday. Red-throated divers at Mill Loch, the vast colonies of kittiwake and guillemot on the cliffs, and smaller species in the sheltered areas. There are several hills, in contrast to Sanday and North Ronaldsay. Ward Hill is the highest, at 334ft., and there is a panoramic view from the top. Eday means isthmus island, and there is less than half a mile between Fersness Bay in the west, and the Bay of London in the east. The cultivated area of the island is not great, compared to the total area, but the heather moorland with its extensive deposits of peat was the source of Eday's prosperity in the past. This fuel was exported to peatless islands, and in the nineteenth century quantities were sold to whisky distilleries all over Scotland. Highland Park Whisky, founded in Kirkwall around 1798, is still using peat, which imparts a unique flavour to the drink.

There are many megalithic remains, especially the chambered cairn at Huntersquoy, which is two-storey, one cairn above the other. Only one other such cairn has been discovered, at Taiversoe Tuick in Rousay. There is a stalled cairn near Sandyhill Smith, excavated in 1937. Eday shares with Rousay the greatest density of chambered cairns in Orkney. At Mill Loch there is one of the island's three standing stones, the Stone of Setter, a mighty lichened sandstone block like a gigantic hand. There are several burnt mounds, at Backland, Quarryhouse, and Greentoft.

Much of the island belongs to Carrick House, in the north of Eday. At the beginning of the seventeenth century James Stewart, second son of Earl Robert Stewart, was created Earl of Carrick, and it was he who built Carrick House. The dating stone of 1633 is still above the door. A later owner, James Fea of Whitehall, in Stronsay, was responsible for the capture of Pirate Gow, and the bell of Gow's ship, the *Revenge*, is within the house.

Eday has a resident doctor, and a primary school. There is an island community co-operative shop.

Access: By air twice daily, Mon. – Sat.
Loganair Ltd., Kirkwall Airport. Tel. (0856) 2494.
By sea thrice weekly from Kirkwall.
Orkney Islands Shipping Co. Ltd., Kirkwall. Tel. (0856) 2044.

STRONSAY

This peaceful island consists of three large sections, divided by gently formed bays, with beautiful sandy beaches. Stronsay is low-lying, especially in the south-east. From Lamb Head in the south to Odin Ness in the north, there are bird-rich cliffs. There is a spectacular gloup in the south-east, called Vat of Kirbuster, and nearby Brough is a nesting place for puffins. Rothiesholm Head is an excellent cliff for seabirds. At the east of the Bay of Houseby, on Stronsay's south coast, is a broch, and there is a cairn at the west of the bay.

Large two-storeyed houses are grouped around the pierhead, in the north, sheltered by the small isle of Papa Stronsay. The village of Whitehall was once occupied by fishermen, at the time of the herring boom, when Stronsay was the most important herring station in the North Isles. A fleet of up to five hundred boats supplied fifteen fish curing stations at Whitehall, and five on Papa Stronsay. Fifteen hundred women were employed at the height of the season. Dutch fishermen came to Stronsay as they did to Shetland. Whaling was an important source of oil and revenue. After the demise of the herring industry, fishing in Stronsay also went into decline, and now it gives work to only a few people.

Three-quarters of a mile south of the village of Whitehall is the old well of Kildinguie, once believed to cure every disease except bubonic plague.

In 1722 James Fea of Whitehall introduced the collection of seaweed for the production of kelp. Kelp kilns can still be seen on the shores, where the seaweed was burned to produce ash, essential for the production of alum, soap, glass, and for bleaching. Kelp eventually became a major part of the island's economy, until its collapse in 1832. Now the rearing of beef cattle on large, modern well-run farms is Stronsay's main industry.

To the south of Stronsay is the island of Auskerry, with its automatic lighthouse. Sheep are pastured here in summer, and a standing stone, a prehistoric grave, and the ruin of a chapel, show that people once lived on Auskerry. Linga Holm on Stronsay's north-west coast has been acquired by the Rare Breeds Survival Trust, and a healthy, thriving flock of North

Ronaldsay native sheep has been established, in case disease or pollution should wipe out the sheep in North Ronaldsay.

Stronsay has a resident doctor, a primary and a junior secondary school. There is a hotel in the village.

Access: By air from Kirkwall twice or thrice daily, Mon. – Sat.
Loganair Ltd., Kirkwall Airport. Tel. (0856) 2494.
By sea thrice weekly from Kirkwall.
Orkney Islands Shipping Co. Ltd., Kirkwall. Tel. (0856) 2044.

ROUSAY

This island is one of the most interesting in Orkney, and unlike any other in the group. Almost circular in shape, and six miles across, the centre is high, with wide tracts of heathery moorland. There are large trout lochs, with some of the best fishing in the islands. From the summit of Blotchnie Fiold, 821 ft. and from Ward and Kierfea Hills, there are spectacular views as far north as Fair Isle, and south into Caithness, as well as over the islands, Eynhallow, Egilsay and Wyre. Rare birds, like the Hen Harrier and Peregrine Falcon hunt here. To the west and north, there are cliff walks to Scabra Head and Sacquoy Head, rising to 200 ft. Hellia Spur on the north-west corner is one of Europe's most important seabird colonies. Gulls, razorbills and guillemots breed here among the unusual rock formations, and puffins haunt the cliffs.

The main road in Rousay encircles the island, parallel with the coast, and most of the houses are gathered round the road, especially around the Sound between Mainland and Egilsay. Here the coast is low, and the land goes right down to the shore. There are seals to be seen in the water around the island, and the waters are rich in fish.

Rousay has been called the 'Egypt of the North', because of the profusion of ancient monuments, of which more than two hundred are registered. It is awe-inspiring to contemplate the presence of so much evidence of the past. In the west of the island is Midhowe, 'the great ship of death', a magnificent stalled cairn, excavated in the 1930s at the expense of W.G. Grant, the whisky magnate. Midhowe is 76 ft. long, and divided into twelve compartments by pairs of transverse upright slabs of stone. The skeletons of twenty-five people were found here, with the remains of sheep, cattle and deer.

Taiversoe Tuick is a Neolithic, two storey, chambered cairn, each at one time having a separate entrance, like Huntersquoy in Eday. The remains of skeletons were found on the shelves of both chambers, together with some cremated bones. Nearby is the Blackhammer chambered tomb, of contemporary date, covered by an oblong mound, with a long passage divided by upright slabs. In the smaller stalled cairn, Knowe of Yarso, twenty more people were buried, with the remains of animals, including thirty deer. At Knowe of Lairso is a most unusual 'horned' cairn.

Eynhallow Sound is bordered by many brochs, and the best preserved is Midhowe Broch, where many implements, including some of Roman origin, were found. At Westness a Viking site is being excavated. A Norse cemetery was discovered when a farmer was burying a cow. He came across the grave of a high-born woman, buried with her infant. The silver brooches interred with her are in the Royal Museum of Scotland, Queen St., Edinburgh.

Beside the Geo of Skaill is the ruin of a medieval chapel, with a stone aumbry in the wall. Near it is an abandoned village, occupied until the middle of last century. Rousay is an island where past meets present, and where the veil which obscures other times is thinly stretched.

Westness House and chapel, with its gardens, are not open to the public at present. There is a hotel and guest houses, two shops, and a craft shop and restaurant at the pier. The fish processing factory also welcomes visitors. Rousay has a resident doctor and a primary school.

Access: By sea, frequent daily service from Tingwall Jetty, Evie.
Orkney Islands Shipping Co. Ltd.
Ferry Office, Tingwall, Evie. Tel. Evie 360.

EGILSAY

This interesting island, one mile east of Rousay, is about three miles long, and one mile across at its widest point. It is shaped like an arrow head. In its lochs and marshes there are many species of birds and water fowl.

Egilsay has played a large part in the history of Orkney, prominent in *The Orkneyinga Saga*, and in modern Orkney literature. The martyrdom of St. Magnus took place here in Easter week, 1116. Magnus and his cousin, Earl Hakon Paulsson, each ruled part of Orkney, but because of ill-feeling brought about by trouble-makers, disputes arose. Through the treachery of Earl Hakon, Magnus and his followers were caught in a trap, at what was to have been a reconciliation between the cousins, in Egilsay. Hakon arrived with a large force of men, and several ships, instead of two ships and an agreed number of men.

Magnus was killed by a mighty blow from an axe wielded by Hakon's cook, after his standard bearer had refused to carry out the execution. Magnus died bravely, and was buried at Birsay, at the church built by his grandfather, Earl Thorfinn. Hakon reformed after the killing, and went on a pilgrimage to the Holy Land. A stone marks the spot where Magnus died.

Egilsay's most important feature is the church of St. Magnus, built on a low central ridge. Its high round tower, believed to be Irish in its inspiration, is 48ft. high, and was at least 15ft. higher. The nave is 30ft. long, and the chancel 15ft. and barrel-vaulted. The walls are massive, with decorative stone blocks, and the high tower, unique in Orkney, can be seen for miles.

Bishop William the Old may well have had his residence in Egilsay, and it is probable that he instigated the building of the church, dedicated to St. Magnus.

Egilsay's small population continues to farm the island, and there is a primary school.

Access: By sea, frequent daily service from Tingwall Jetty, Evie.
Orkney Islands Shipping Co. Ltd.
Ferry Office, Tingwall, Evie. Tel. Evie 360.

WYRE

Wyre, so called because it is shaped like an arrow-head, Old Norse *vigr*, is situated between Gairsay and Rousay. It is two miles long by three-quarters of a mile wide, and there are eight farms.

Like Egilsay, Wyre has had a dramatic and exciting past. The great Viking chieftain, Kolbein Hruga, who is mentioned in *The Orkneyinga Saga* as being 'the most haughty of men', built his castle here. Known as Cubbie Roo's Castle, it has a square keep surrounded by a ditch, and there are traces of an upper floor, ground chamber, and water tank. The castle, a 'safe stronghold', was the refuge of Snaekill Gunnason, who fled there after killing John, last of the Viking Earls, in 1232.

Kolbein belonged to one of the mightiest Norse families, and his castle must have been an important fortification, capable of withstanding the attacks of a powerful enemy force. Bjarni, the son of Kolbein, was the third Bishop of Orkney, 1188-1223, and he was one of the greatest personalities and poets of his time. Bishop Bjarni founded Kirkwall Grammar School, one of the most ancient foundations in Britain, and the school drew its revenue from land in Wyre. Bjarni furthered the building of St. Magnus Cathedral, and influenced the canonisation of Earl Rognvald in 1192.

It is believed that the small romanesque chapel near the castle was built by Kolbein for his son. It is roofless, but partially restored.

Edwin Muir, Orkney's famous poet and writer, spent part of his childhood on the Island of Wyre, at the farm of Bu. This farm name shows that it was the house of the island's most prominent family, and no doubt it was Kolbein's farm. Edwin Muir describes his early and happy life in his autobiography.

Wyre today is a quiet island, with acres of uncultivated heather moorland for the bird watcher and naturalist to explore.

Access: By sea, frequent daily service from Tingwall Jetty, Evie.
Orkney Islands Shipping Co. Ltd.
Ferry Office, Tingwall, Evie. Tel. Evie 360.

GAIRSAY

Gairsay lies between Shapinsay and Rousay, and is one and three quarters of a mile wide. Its highest point in 334ft., and there is a good view of the surrounding islands from the summit. To the south and east there is good fertile land, but no cultivation to the north and east.

Gairsay's claim to fame is that it was once the stronghold of a great Viking pirate chief, Sweyn Asleifsson of Langskaill. The foundations of his magnificent sixty-foot drinking hall are believed to be under the present seventeenth century house, and it is likely that Millburn Bay was the anchorage for his ships. Sweyn spent his summers plundering down the west coast of Scotland, and Ireland, and had a reputation for incredible bravery as well as for violence. In winter he returned to Gairsay with his booty, to carouse with his followers, and live on the island's farm produce. In spite of his piracy, the earls of Orkney and the kings of Scotland were his friends.

It was on his last expedition to Ireland that Sweyn and his Vikings died in a trap, for the Irish, still seething from his previous visit, had dug pits inside the gates of the town that Sweyn and his men were about to attack. Sweyn and his followers were killed in the ensuing fight, a fitting end for a pirate.

In 1640, Gairsay was acquired by the wealthy Craigie family, and Sir William Craigie, landowner and MP, was one of the most powerful and astute Orcadians of his century. He built his fortified mansion on the site of Sweyn Asleifsson's hall, reconstructing a late sixteenth century house, with the addition of a new wing, a bowling green and a sunken garden. The Craigies owned town houses in Kirkwall, and all of Wyre and Gairsay, as well as estates on Sanday, Stronsay, Rousay and Rendall.

Only one family still lives in Gairsay, farming Langskaill, which still has its courtyard and arched gateway, above which Sir William Craigie inscribed his motto, *Timor Omnis Abest*—Dread Nought. The only communication with the island is by boat, which brings in supplies, and is the family's transport to the Mainland.

SHAPINSAY

This island is only twenty-five minutes by daily passenger boat from Kirkwall. Its rich and fertile soil, and well-managed farms produce the splendid beef cattle for which Shapinsay is famous. Because it is so near the Mainland, its tranquil beaches are easily reached, and there are many interesting and rewarding walks. As in the other islands, there is a rich and varied bird life, and large breeding colonies of gull and tern. Seals bask on the beaches and skerries, and can be seen from the Galt at the north-west tip, as well as elsewhere on the shores. The Ouse and Lairo Water are well worth a walk, and from the top of the Ward Hill, 210ft., there is a memorable view.

The uninhabited island of Helliar Holm, with its lighthouse, cairn, broch and chapel site, lies to the right of the approach to Shapinsay Pier. It was in Elwick Bay, which shelters the pier, that King Hakon's fleet of a hundred ships lay at anchor in 1263, before the Battle of Largs. Balfour Village, along the west side of the bay, was built in the early nineteenth century by Col. David Balfour to house craftsmen. He also built a large water-powered mill half-a-mile outside the village, one of the finest examples of its kind.

Col. David Balfour of Balfour and Trenabie was the heir of John Balfour, a typical nabob, who made a fortune in India, acquired lands, and became MP for Orkney and Shetland in 1790. He owned much of the island of Shapinsay, and began the building of magnificent Balfour Castle, completed by David Balfour in 1848. It is a fascinating building, set in the south-west corner of the island, against a background of trees, unusual in Orkney, and it contains family heirlooms and other treasures.

David Balfour was an improver, and it was he who squared off the fields into ten-acre units, and separated them by drainage ditches. He had straight roads laid out, and revolutionised agriculture in the island, increasing production tenfold. He introduced modern farming methods, and he was also a writer and a historian, interested in Orkney's colourful and exciting past.

The father of Washington Irving was born at Quholme in Shapinsay, and emigrated to the United States. There are many interesting archaeological sites, mostly unexcavated, and permission can be obtained to inspect them. The standing stone, Mor Stein, Castle Bloody, a chambered cairn, Odin's Stone, Dishan Tower, and the Broch of Burroughston are all interesting to visit.

A thriving and progressive community, with much to see and do, Shapinsay has a resident doctor and a primary school. Boats are built by a local boat builder in the premises of the old school.

Access: By sea daily from Kirkwall.
Orkney Islands Shipping Co. Ltd., Kirkwall. Tel. (0856) 2044.

GRAEMSAY

This small island, two miles long and three-quarters of a mile wide, lies in a most beautiful situation, between Hoy and Stromness. It is green and peaceful, and still completely unspoiled. There are two lighthouses on the island and some farms.

Access: By sea from Stromness once a week on Wed.
Orkney Islands Shipping Co. Ltd., Kirkwall. Tel. (0856) 2044.
Also thrice weekly from Stromness.
Mr. S. Mowat, Barkland, Cairston Rd., Stromness. Tel. (0856) 850 624.

HOY

Hoy has a right to its name, high island in O.N., for it is a mountainous island in a low-lying archipelago. The second largest island in Orkney, it is thirteen miles long, and has the highest hill, Ward Hill, at 1565ft. Much of Hoy is high moorland, with lochs and burns. In the east the land slopes down gently to Scapa Flow, where the coastline is low, and more densely inhabited than the rest of the island.

Hoy's high west coast of flaming red sandstone cliffs is uninhabited until the deep valley of Rackwick is reached, a spectacular and awe-inspiring bay between Ward Hill, Moor Fea and Mel Fea. North from Rackwick is a route to the Old Man of Hoy, a familiar sight to all those who come to Orkney across the Pentland Firth. This high stack, 450ft., was climbed in 1966, and subsequent climbs were televised. Aeons of breakers and storms have pounded the Old Man, who withstands their onslaughts undisturbed.

Further out to the north, the coast is even more magnificent. St. John's Head, one of the highest perpendicular cliffs in Britain, rivalling even St. Kilda, rises sheer above the sea to more than 1000ft. Views from St. John's

Head, and as far north as Braebuster, are dizzying and breath-taking, as vast colonies of seabirds wheel and heckle above the turbulent water, and the distant mountains of northern Scotland, as well as the rest of Orkney and Shetland can be seen.

Hoy has been designated a Site of Special Scientific Interest, because of the variety of birds that nest on the island. Red-throated divers, Arctic Skuas and Great Skuas, as well as Peregrine Falcons and Manx Shearwaters shelter here, as well as many smaller species. Rare alpine flowers, not found elsewhere in Orkney, grow in the tracts near Knap of Trowieglen. In Berriedale, a sheltered place between the hills, is Orkney's only indigenous wood, with birks, hazel, poplar, ash and other varieties. Insects and small animals find a comfortable habitat, and grasshoppers can sometimes be heard in summer. The mountain hare lopes in the hills.

One of Orkney's most mysterious and well-known prehistoric monuments is sited near Rackwick, the great megalithic Dwarfie Stane, a chambered tomb carved out of a solid block of red sandstone. There are two cells, entered by a passage, and the stone is the subject of legend and superstition. A more modern relic is the naval base of Lyness, one of Britain's most important bases during World War II. Thirty thousand men were stationed here when Scapa Flow was used by the Royal Navy.

There is a ferry terminal and air strip in South Walls, where there is a thriving farming community. Walls forms the southern part of the island, divided by the inlet of Longhope in the east, and North Bay in the west. Hoy is an island unlike any other in Orkney, beautiful and dramatic, where even the climate seems different from that in the other low green islands, rising gently out of the northern sea.

There is a doctor on the island, a school, and many places of interest to visit, including historic Melsetter House.

Access: By sea, frequent daily service from Houton, Orphir, to Lyness, Hoy. Orkney Islands Shipping Co. Ltd. Tel. Orphir 397.
A private service operates daily from Stromness.
Mr. S. Mowat, Stromness. Tel. (0856) 850 624.

FLOTTA

Although it is only three-quarters of a mile from the hilly island of Hoy, Flotta is completely different. Its name means flat island, in O.N., and it is indeed flat, and about three miles long by two miles wide. This island, one of the quietest in Orkney, was heavily fortified during both World Wars, and the batteries can still be seen.

Flotta has assumed great importance in the economy of Britain, since it became an oil terminal in 1977. The island has good harbour facilities, and there are usually large tankers lying off the south of Scapa Flow. Oil is piped to Flotta from the Piper and Claymore Fields in the North Sea, and stored in seven huge storage tanks, before being shipped away for processing. The huge flare of burning petroleum gas can be seen for miles, lighting up the sky.

Oil developments have been successfully contained in Flotta, thus ensuring that Orkney benefits from increased income and jobs, while avoiding the serious disruption to the traditional way of life which otherwise might occur.

Access: By sea, frequent daily service.
Orkney Islands Shipping Co. Ltd., Houton. Tel. Orphir 397.

BURRAY AND SOUTH RONALDSAY

The eastern group of the South Isles is linked to the Mainland by the Churchill Barriers, which were built between the islands of Glims Holm, Burray and South Ronaldsay. These giant concrete blocks, each between five and ten tons, were dropped into the water to close the eastern approaches to

Scapa Flow, after the sinking of the battleship *Royal Oak*, in October 1939. Later an excellent road was constructed along the top of the barriers.

The Italian prisoners of war who made the blocks built a small chapel on Lamb Holm from two Nissen huts. The chapel, still used and visited by thousands of people over the years, is beautifully appointed and carefully maintained. The prisoners used whatever materials they could obtain, including the metal from bully-beef tins, and the altar has a painting above it done by one of the prisoners from a reproduction of Nicolo Barabino's *As a fair olive tree in the plains.* The chapel is a poignant example of triumph of creativity, and a memorial of those years of war.

The Island of Burray is most attractive, and extensively farmed. There are golden sandy bays and impressive cliff walks. The shores are rich in seabirds of many kinds, and Ness is a bird sanctuary well worth seeing. The small, nearbye island of Hunda is especially noteworthy, in particular for its breeding sites. Seals come close in to the shores and barriers, and otters too can be seen at night. In these islands are Orkney's most prolific shell-fish beaches. Copper was once mined at the Wha Taing, near Hunda.

In the village of Burray there is a boat builders' yard, owned by the same family for several generations. Both islands were extremely active and prosperous during the herring boom.

South Ronaldsay, joined to Burray by barrier, is also unspoiled, beautiful and fertile. It is farmed extensively, and there are farms all over the island. St. Margaret's Hope, a village of silver-grey, two-storey houses, shelters in a bay. It was named after the young Norwegian princess, Margaret, who died in 1290, during a stormy journey to Scotland and a marriage which would have made her queen of Scotland and England. Her ship sought refuge here.

Visit the Orkney Wireless Museum in Church Road where you can see a collection showing wartime defences and radio at Scapa Flow. It also features domestic radio and handiwork of Italian prisoners of war during their internment in Orkney.

The cliffs on the east rise to 200ft., and colonies of seabirds throng the ledges. All along the coast are small sandy bays, where seals swim in the clear water. From the top of Ward Hill there are views far south across the firth into Scotland.

As in the other islands, there are fascinating glimpses of a strange and colourful past. One of the most intriguing is the mysterious Tomb of the Eagles, a stalled chamber cairn, dating from 3000 BC. Among the human remains there were found the claws of many sea eagles, perhaps indicating the burial place of some important chief or family. The tomb is near Liddle Farm, where Mr. Simison (Tel. St. Margaret's Hope 339) is willing to show visitors the significance of the site and the burnt mound nearbye.

At Northfield in Burray there are the remains of a broch, and at Hoxa Head in the north-west of South Ronaldsay a Viking burial was found near the ruin of a broch. This burial is on the exact site mentioned in *The Orkneyinga Saga* as being the spot where Thorfinn Skullsplitter was buried.

At St. Mary's Church, in one of the most beautiful places in South Ronaldsay, there is a remarkable relic in the shape of an ancient block of stone, with the carved impression of a pair of feet. There are the remains of other early chapels on the islands.

A modern development is the Hydro Board's experimental windmill at Berriedale, which contributes to the national grid. It's well worth visiting. An agricultural museum; the block ships sunk at the causeway at the beginning of the Second World War; the many arts and crafts practised in the islands; as well as traditional events such as the unique Boys' Ploughing Match, and Festival of the Horse, in August, give Burray and South Ronaldsay a special position in the popularity of the islands.

Access: By the main road from Kirkwall via Holm.

History on Show

Bryce Wilson, Museums Officer, O.I.C.

TANKERNESS HOUSE MUSEUM, Broad St., Kirkwall.
(O.I.C. Museums Service)

This museum provides a vivid introduction to Orkney's numerous and spectacular pre-historic remains. A permanent exhibition, *The First Settlers,* portrays life in the Neolithic and Bronze Age, with examples of tools and weapons dating back 5,000 years. From Isbister, 'The Tomb of the Eagles', come skeletal remains of some of our earliest inhabitants and part of the largest hoard of Neolithic pottery from any one site in Scotland: from the remains of a Neolithic tomb in Westray comes a magnificent spiral-carved stone, which parallels those found in the Boyne Valley of Ireland. From the Bronze Age there are spear and axe-heads, and burial urns of steatite and clay.

The Iron Age with its impressive defensive brochs is represented by the finds from the Howe excavation, among them the unique Insect Brooch and many fine examples of pottery.

Orkney's Pictish culture is represented by the Burrian Symbol Stone and the finds from the Buckquoy excavation, which leads on to the Norse exhibits, among them fine brooch moulds from Birsay and combs from Skaill in Deerness. A plain wooden box which once contained the bones of St. Magnus, now in their final resting place in the cathedral, is also on view.

Tankerness House, with its crow-stepped gables and sandstone mouldings, has been described as one of the finest vernacular town houses in Scotland. Originally the domain of the cathedral clergy in the 16th century, it was acquired by the Baikies of Tankerness in the early 17th century, to be the town house of this family of merchant lairds for more than 300 years. It was acquired by Kirkwall Town Council in the 1950's and restored as a museum in 1968. It is now the headquarters of O.I.C.'s Museums Service.

Open all year, Mon. – Sat. 10.30 – 12.30, 1.30 – 5.00. Open on Sunday May – Sept., 2.00 – 5.00. Admission £1.00, April – Sept. Free to O.A.P.'s, the unemployed, children and students. Wheelchairs ground floor only.

STROMNESS MUSEUM, 52 Alfred Street, Stromness.
(Orkney Natural History Society)

Nearing the southern end of Stromness's tortuous main street is one of the most remarkable small museums in Scotland. Since it was founded in 1837 by the Orkney Natural History Society it has built up important collections on Orkney's Natural and Maritime History.

Since 1974, a main feature of the ground-floor Maritime Gallery has been a display on the German High Seas Fleet which after the First World War was scuttled in Scapa Flow. The display and accompanying booklet have done much to encourage the growing sub-aqua industry, which brings hundreds to Orkney each year to dive on the remains of the Fleet in what is considered one of the best diving areas in the world.

During the eighteenth and nineteenth centuries the ships of the Hudson's Bay Company called at Stromness to pick up workers for the company's trading posts in Canada. The displays and archives at Stromness Museum recall many of these, including Dr. John Rae, who, as a company explorer, virtually completed the mapping of Northern Canada and discovered the fate of the Franklin Expedition.

Other visitors were the whalers of Hull and Dundee which carried Orkney crewmen in search of the Greenland whale, and Captain Cook's ships which made Stromness their first British landfall after his death in the Pacific. There are also displays on local craft, boat building, the Lifeboat, inshore fishing and the Herring Fishing Boom, along with an extensive photograph collection on Stromness and district.

The Natural History Gallery houses one of Scotland's best collections of stuffed birds, local bird's eggs, the Robert Rendall collection of Orkney Shells and seaweeds, the Magnus Spence Herbarium of Orkney plants, the Lorimer collection of Orkney butterflies and moths, local fossils and geological samples, and a small archaeological display chiefly from Skara Brae.

The collections are housed in a charming nineteenth century building which used to be Stromness's Town Hall. It is picturesquely situated on one of the small piers that line the harbour, and is well worth the ten minute walk from the Pier Head.

Open all year, 10.30 – 12.30, 1.30 – 5.00. Mon. – Sat.
Open on public holidays. Closed on Sunday and three weeks in Feb.
Admission: Adults 30p. Children 10p. Schools free.
Wheelchairs ground floor only.

THE ORKNEY FARM & FOLK MUSEUM
(O.I.C. Museums Service)
Kirbuster, Birsay. (A986 N.W. from Dounby)
Corrigall, Harray. (A986 S.W. from Dounby)

This museum occupies two historic farmsteads in Orkney's West Mainland, and has a special place in Orkney's predominantly agricultural community. Here are portrayed the life and traditions of many generations of Orcadians, at the same time showing that change, however slow, has always been part of island life.

At Kirbuster, we see the ancient 'firehoose', a feature of Orkney farmhouses until the 19th century. The hearth is in the middle of the room, built against a low stone wall or 'back'. Smoke from the peat fire escapes through the wooden smoke-hole or 'lum'. Cooking pots are suspended by a hook and chain from an oak beam called the 'pauntree'. Beyond the hearth is accommodation for calves.

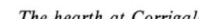

The hearth at Corrigall

The improvements of the 19th century can be seen at Corrigall, where an intrusive stone gable incorporates the hearth, and cooking pots hang from an iron 'swey'.

The simple furnishings of both farmhouses include straw-backed stools and baskets of straw or heather, spinning equipment and meal girnels, and a kirn for brewing ale. Salted fish and pork hang from the rafters.

The principal feature of the restored barn at Corrigall is the circular grain-drying kiln. Here, crops of bere and oats were threshed with flails on the hard clay floor before drying in the kiln and grinding into meal on the quern or at the parish mill. During the winter, straw ropes were made in the barn for thatching, binding stacks and general use on the farm.

The large stable attached to the barn was built in the 19th century to accommodate the heavy horse then introduced to cope with the increasing mechanisation of farm work. A growing collection of horse-drawn farm machinery is displayed under cover at Kirbuster, and in the area around the farm buildings at Corrigall.

Popular features of the Farm and Folk Museum are the examples of native sheep, poultry and other livestock.

Open April – Sept., 10.30 – 1.00, 2.00 – 5.00. Sun. 2.00 – 7.00. Admission £1.00 which includes both sites. Free to O.A.P.'s, the unemployed, children and students. Wheelchairs throughout.

Folk at Work

Alan Coghill, Industrial Development Officer O.I.C.

The lush grasslands of Orkney give some indication of the historical importance of agriculture to the economy of the islands. Farmers have kept abreast of modern methods, and mechanisation has resulted in reduced employment. Growing from the need to replace this has been a wide diversification of activity ranging from the production of food products, whisky, confectionery, a large variety of crafts and knitwear, a thriving fishing industry in pelagic, whitefish and shellfish species, fish farming of salmon and shellfish and the now well established oil handling terminal on the island of Flotta in Scapa Flow.

Many changes have taken place in agriculture over the last few years although the main emphasis remains on the production of beef and dairy cattle. Sheep, too, have been an important factor and the production of seed potatoes another feature.

Several food units directly utilise the products of the agriculture industry, the most important being the abattoir on the Kirkwall industrial estate and the creamery operated by the North of Scotland Milk Marketing Board, which has won numerous awards in recent years. A small unit at Swannay Farms in Birsay also produces quality cheese. Other small businesses utilise the meat and fish products to produce pâté and there is a small potato crisp factory.

There are a number of bakeries specialising in the production of the well known Orkney oatcakes and biscuits, and these are becoming popular throughout the U.K. In Stromness, there is a factory producing Orkney fudge which, like most Orkney products, has gained its reputation from the quality of its product. The two distilleries are located on the outskirts of Kirkwall and produce high quality malt whisky. The largest and best known is the Highland Park Distillery which was founded in 1798 and the second is the Scapa Distillery. In 1988, the Orkney Brewery was established and now produces 'Raven Ale'.

Fishing has developed considerably in recent years, although the fleet is small in number, it boasts modern vessels in the pelagic, white fish and shellfish sector, and Orkney vessels are prominent among the top earners of the Scottish fleet. Orkney has long been renowned for its shellfish products including lobsters, crabmeat and scallops for export to Europe and this has been complemented in the last year by the direct transport of these and more exotic species, e.g. velvet crab, to the south of Europe by vivier lorry. Several small factories also handle shellfish and these are located in Westray, Rousay, Kirkwall and Stronsay. Some are of vital strategic importance in that they provide employment and stability in the remoter areas. White fish landings increased five fold between 1981 and 1987, a tribute to the ability and development of the fleet.

Complementing the fishing industry has been the growth of fish farming of salmon and shellfish. There are now fourteen salmon farms and ten shellfish units. This has given rise to the development of a number of small businesses utilising these products. These include sales of fresh and smoked salmon and shellfish and feature some unique delicatessen products. A small firm producing marinated herring has expanded in the last few years and has had a positive impact on the market.

Knitwear, too, provides employment throughout the islands, comprising fifteen firms of variable size, employing 600-700 knitters in their homes. The larger firms are located in Kirkwall and Sanday but the others are well spread throughout the islands producing a range from traditional design to modern and high fashion garments, both hand-machine and hand-knitted. Recently, appreciation has been expressed of the high standard of production and fashion awareness of Orkney firms. A large proportion of the companies are represented by the Orkney Knitwear Trades Association for marketing purposes. In addition, two small firms produce tweed to traditional designs.

A feature of the Orkney scene in recent years has been the growing kaleidoscope of small crafts in the islands and this has been encouraged by the Council and to a degree by Orkney Craftsmen's Guild. Unique to the islands is the production of the Orkney chair using traditional methods and the Orkney bridescog. The largest producers are the two silver and goldsmiths who are now among the principal producers of silver and gold jewellery in the U.K. Between them they employ over seventy people and export extensively, as well as selling to every corner of the U.K. Pottery is also popular and other craftsmen produce sheepskins, toys, woodcrafts, ceramic jewellery, resin sculptures, prints, a range of handcrafted garments and handfelted carpets and wallcoverings. Again the craftspeople are well spread throughout the islands. A woodcarver of international renown has a workshop in Kirkwall.

The tourist industry has grown in significance and importance in recent years. The 850th Anniversary of St. Magnus Cathedral in 1987 was expected to be a peak year but the number of visitors has continued to increase. Orkney is particularly well served by small restaurants and can boast that the fare is of high quality and good value. Orcadians have a well established reputation for first class hospitality.

The only major industry established in Orkney in recent years has been the oil handling terminal on the island of Flotta in Scapa Flow. The terminal was constructed by the Occidental consortium initially to handle oil from the Piper field some 100 miles east of Wick. The base was opened in 1977 and shortly afterwards the Claymore field was included. The Tartan field, which is operated by Texaco, was also connected to the facilities and has since been joined by several smaller satellite fields. The terminal itself contains five half-million and two one-million gallon crude oil storage tanks, a gas storage and liquefication plant, a deballast treatment plant and storage tanks, together with the other facilities required for this type of depot. As a result of a close relationship with the many environmental bodies, the impact on the local scene has been minimised.

The Land

Peter Leith

The land in Orkney has been farmed for five thousand years.

The earliest settlers came by sea to farm along the shores. They ornamented their pottery with impressions of the four-rowed barley that was their precious crop. They harvested the grain, making it into meal or malt as occasion demanded. This grain is still grown to a limited extent, but has been largely replaced by modern hybrid higher yielding barley.

As time passed, farming the land and tending the cattle and sheep became more important than hunting the shore and the sea. Gradually they pushed their boundaries further up the hills, increasing the acreage under cultivation to try to avoid the shortages that came when bad weather spoiled a harvest.

Since then invasions both violent and peaceful have changed the style of government and the people. Newcomers brought new ideas that became part of the farming scene.

The improvement in communications made the biggest change in farming. When the foods of the world became available to everybody, Orkney's farming changed from growing grain to feed itself to producing high quality meat for the large urban centres.

Modern agriculture in Orkney is based on good utilisation of grass, used to feed high quality sheep and cattle. During summer the animals graze the fields and the surplus is conserved for winter feed, mostly in the form of silage. The green grass is tightly compressed to exclude all air and is thus preserved in an inert state until needed as stockfeed.

Less hay is made than silage. Most of it is now baled, but as it is air dried it is much more at risk in the rather variable Orkney climate.

The northern maritime climate is mild, favouring the growth of grass in summer, but in winter the land is too wet for cattle and they must be housed. The growing season starts around the first of May and is on average about 230 days—a month less than in south-west Scotland.

The soil is derived from the old red sandstone rock that forms the foundations of the Islands and tends to be acidic. In some parts, notably on the Island of Sanday, there is sandy soil, rich in lime.

Most of the farms are owner-occupied. Some are large, but the majority are less than 150 acres. The expense of modern machinery is encouraging the setting up of larger units where there are economies of scale.

Over the years the farm buildings have been changed from the old thatched, humid, unhealthy kind, to the modern more open type. They may not be so picturesque but they are healthier for the animals and much more convenient for the farmer.

Farmland at Marwick

Most of the farming income comes from the sale of beef cattle, traditionally the black Aberdeen-Angus, with Shorthorn and some white-faced Herefords. Recently Continental breeds like Charolais and Simmental have been introduced making the herds colourful with their red and fawn coats. The majority of the young animals are sent to be fattened nearer the large urban centres, but recently a processing plant has been established near Kirkwall to pack the meat for supermarket sale. A steady trade with two supermarket chains has already been established.

The industry works under the difficulties imposed by long distance from the commercial centres. This adds to the cost of such things as fertilisers and machinery and deducts a percentage from the sale of produce. The outer islands have a double disadvantage with extra charges on the inter-island ferries. A third of Orkney's cattle are on these islands.

A sizeable dairy section supplies the local demand for milk, the surplus being processed at the factory in Kirkwall into a high quality cheese that has won top awards in national competition.

Sheep remain in the open all year, the main breeds being North Country Cheviot and Border Leicester. The wool is sheared in summer and, although knitting is a flourishing local industry, there is no local spinning mill.

The native sheep that live on the shore in North Ronaldsay are an interesting relic from the past, but have little commercial value. They are classed as one of the rare breeds of the world.

About a tenth of the arable acreage is cropped for stock feed, two-thirds being barley, the rest oats. The old labour-intensive methods of cutting and stooking the sheaves have mostly given way to cutting by combine harvester and the moist grain is preserved with propionic acid.

A significant acreage of potatoes can be grown for top grade seed, as the cool northern climate is a factor in the control of disease.

Throughout the years, generations of skilled farmers have used the land's resources for the benefit of the community. The history of a race is not in the quarrels of its Princes, but in the achievements of its people.

The Sea

William Jolly

The sea around Orkney has always been a vital part of the Orcadian way of life. It has provided the inhabitants of these islands with food, and has been a cradle for thousands of fine seamen.

Line fishing for tusk, cod and ling was probably first practised in Orkney early in the eighteenth century. The fish were split, salted and left to dry by the womenfolk, who tended them, stacked them, and covered them with tarpaulins every night and when it rained. Most of these fish were exported to Spain, N. Africa and the Argentine.

Fishing was good throughout the islands, tusk being more valuable than ling, and cod fetching the lowest price, owing to the texture of its flesh and keeping qualities. Fish caught and dry-salted in the North Isles of Orkney in 1840 amounted to: Westray 120 tons; Eday 109 tons; Stronsay 30 tons; Shapinsay 65 tons; North Ronaldsay 10 tons; Sanday 20 tons; Rousay and adjacent isles 90 tons. A total of 440 tons for which the fishermen received £5400.

A herring fishing industry was started in Stronsay by Mr. David Drever of Huip Farm in 1814 and continued until 1936. A village and a pier were built

The modern purse-trawler Orcades Viking II of Stromness

by Mr. Lang of Papdale in Kirkwall, who was encouraged in this venture by a London firm. At that time, the Stronsay herring fishing commenced about the second week in July and continued for six to eight weeks. It employed as many as 400 sail boats, each with a crew of three to five men. There were also 25 to 30 sloops and brigs anchored at Stronsay, attending to the fishing boats, and there were several hundred women employed in gutting and salting. The average catch was 35 to 70 crans per boat; the largest catch recorded being 200 crans for one boat.

In Stromness, a herring fishing was started in 1837. The catch that year amounted to 2000 crans, caught by sail boats whose only power was a steam capstan for hauling nets and ropes. The last of these boats left Stromness around 1907. A man in Stromness who was a schoolchild at the time can remember the class being taken by their teacher to witness the end of an era—the Stromness herring fleet sailing down Scapa Flow, back to their home ports on the mainland of Scotland.

There was also a lobster fishing carried on in Stromness. The average annual catch for the twelve years from 1837-49 was 11,622 lobsters. These were shipped to Billingsgate market by well smacks from Gravesend.

A herring fishing in Kirkwall was located on the west side of Carness about a mile outside the town, and in Holm at the south-east end of the village, where a salt and net store can still be seen.

There was now a keen demand for Scottish cured herring on the continent and larger and more efficient boats were built to satisfy these new markets. Previously controlled by the Dutch and now open to the British fleets, these continental markets were extremely important.

During the middle of the nineteenth century, larger and better equipped boats were built on the east coast of Scotland. Fishing harbours were improved in Orkney and new piers built to accommodate the increased size of the fishing fleets. The fishing of tusk, ling and cod was increased, mainly due to the demand from Spain and other Latin countries, including the Argentine, for salt fish, otherwise known as stock-fish.

At the end of the nineteenth century, steam-powered trawlers and drifters became common. Their capacity was enormous, hauling in catches of every kind of fish that came within the scope of their nets.

Gradually, line fishing for cod etc. declined. The small local boats no longer found the shoals of fish that had previously frequented their waters. In Orkney, the Rackwick salted cod which was always in high demand soon became only a memory. Trawlers came into the piers in Orkney in bad weather to gut their catches which consisted of every variety imaginable, even shellfish. There was plenty of fish at the piers, but hardly anything left for the local boats on their traditional grounds.

Seine-netting and ring-netting were introduced between the wars, and both efficiently decimated what remained of the shoals.

The last herring drifter in Orkney was the *Beezaleel*, skippered by J. Bruce, which fished out of Burray until 1936. During the fishing season she also worked from Lerwick, Stronsay, Yarmouth and Lowestoft, moving with the fleet that followed the herring.

For many years, poke-netting for sillocks was carried out around the harbours at Stromness and Kirkwall. These small fish, which develop into saithe, were at one time spread on the land and were a source of manure. In 1936, approximately 600 barrels were filled and taken to Stronsay on a special charter of the *Orcadia* where they were made into fish meal manure.

There have been many views expressed regarding the use of fish to make fish meal, manures, pet foods, etc. Can we afford to use such a valuable source of food on such schemes?

The purse-netting of smaller fish such as pout, sand eel, etc., for such purposes deprives larger fish of their main source of food and they will eventually become so scarce that there will be no fishing industry left to provide food for human beings. This has happened in the last century in Orkney and Shetland to such an extent that the fishing industry and the government urgently need to consider the serious position we are in and take the appropriate action to remedy the situation.

Around 1946-47, the White Fish Authority was constituted and loan and grant schemes introduced which enabled fishermen to acquire new boats. It was a great benefit to local fishermen to have their own boats and fish on a share basis. These locally owned boats provided regular employment for many Orcadians and prevented many of the younger people from emigrating. Hopefully they will still increase in number and create more jobs ashore.

Fishing regulations have recently been amended, hopefully to the benefit of the British fishing fleets.

I was a line fisherman for haddock, halibut, lobster and crab for many years, and I can state with genuine authority that there are very few fish or shellfish to be found in our traditional fishing grounds compared with forty or fifty years ago.

We can no longer afford to squander this important asset, of which, after all, we are merely temporary custodians.

The beach at Warbeth, Stromness

The Old Man of Hoy – not for the inexperienced climber

What's Your Sport?

Alan G. Clouston
Principal Community Education Officer, O.I.C.

BOWLING (Outdoor)
Watergate, Kirkwall.
Ness, Stromness. Tel. (0856) 850 772.
School Road, St. Margaret's Hope, South Ronaldsay.

TENNIS
Kirkwall Grammar School Sports Centre. Tel. (0856) 2364.
Ness, Stromness. Tel. (0856) 850 772.
Dounby School, Dounby. (0856) 77234.
St. Margaret's Hope, South Ronaldsay.
Stromness Academy, Stromness. Tel. (0856) 850660.

RIDING
Garson Farm, Stromness. Tel. (0856) 850304.
Orkney Pony Club Annual Summer Training School. Tel. (0856) 2856.
Orkney Riding Club events. (see local press / posters).

CLIMBING
Since the Old Man of Hoy was first climbed in 1966, parties of rock climbers
have come to tackle this 450ft. column of red sandstone and the adjacent
1140ft. cliff St. John's Head. The Orkney cliffs are subject to severe
weathering and should not be tackled by the inexperienced climber.

SWIMMING
Kirkwall Grammar School. (25m. pool) Tel. (0856) 2364.
Hillside Road, Stromness. (25m. pool) Tel. (0856) 850552.
North Walls Centre, Hoy. (9m. pool) Tel. (0856) 79 246 / 311.

GOLF
Grainbank, Kirkwall. (18-hole). Tel. (0856) 2457.
Ness, Stromness. (18-hole) Tel. (0856) 850772.
Isle of Sanday (9-hole). Isle of Westray (9-hole).

DANCING AND DISCOS
Casablanca, Junction Rd., Kirkwall. Tel. (0856) 5038.
Matchmakers, The Albert Hotel, Kirkwall. Tel. (0856) 2053.
Also at various community centres and hotels. See *The Orcadian* (published every Thursday) for details of local events.

SAILING
The Girnel, Harbour Street, Kirkwall. Dingy sailing clubs at Kirkwall, Stromness, Holm, Burray, South Ronaldsay, Rousay and Pierowall.
MODEL YACHTING at the Peerie Sea, Kirkwall; St. Colm's Club, Sanday and St. Tredwell's Club, Papa Westray.

SNOOKER
The Pavilion, Main St., Kirkwall. Tel. (0856) 2944.

SQUASH
Kirkwall Squash Club, Hatston, Kirkwall. Tel. (0856) 2032.
Stromness Squash Club, Market Green, Stromness.

PUTTING
Brandyquoy Park, Palace Road, Kirkwall. Tel. (0856) 3535 Ext. 2409.
Ness, Stromness. Tel. (0856) 850772.

BADMINTON AND TABLE TENNIS
Kirkwall Grammar School Sports Centre. Tel. (0856) 2364.
Community Centre, Kirkwall. Tel. (0856) 3354.
Community Centre, Stromness. Tel. (0856) 850712.
Stromness Academy, Stromness. Tel. (0856) 850660.
Other community centres are often available as wet weather facilities during the summer months. See local posters.

SUB-AQUA DIVING
In 1919 the German navy scuttled seventy of their vessels in Scapa Flow. Sixty-three have been salvaged for scrap but three battleships and four battle cruisers remain on the sea bed. Sub-aqua enthusiasts have the unique opportunity to explore several warships in the same vicinity in clear water.

SPECTATOR SPORTS
Football, rugby, hockey, motocross, autocross, clay pigeon shooting etc.
Read *The Orcadian* (published every Thursday) for details of local events.

PUBLIC PARKS
Bignold Park, Bignold Park Road, Kirkwall; Brandyquoy Park, Kirkwall; Pickaquoy Park, Kirkwall; Marwick Park, Stromness; Market Green, Stromness.

FISHING
Sea Angling Festivals and boats for hire – information from tourist offices. Orkney inland lochs provide excellent sport for the trout fisher. The Orkney Tourist Fishing Association has facilities at a number of the major lochs. Boats and ghillies available locally. Information from the tourist offices.

FITNESS TRAINING (Multigym)
Kirkwall Grammar School Sports Centre. Tel. (0856) 2364 and Stromness Academy, Stromness. Tel. (0856) 850660. These facilities are only available to the public during school holidays.

Orkney Flora

Bessie Skea

Vegetation varies from one Orkney island to another, and Mainland districts have their own specialities. For example, in Firth and Harray we have primrose areas; in Stenness, much meadowsweet; Deerness has streams running with mimulus; Hoy and Rousay have alpine and arctic species growing at low levels.

Our most famous flower is the *Primula scotica*, an exquisite jewel of a few clifftop areas. Its tiny, vivid purple flower-clusters grow low beneath the wind, on short turf salt-swept by the Atlantic, in company with vernal squill, prunella also in royal purple, birds' foot trefoil, thyme and seapinks, which in certain years colour entire clifftops in solid banks of rose and shell-pink. Also brightening our shores are white marguerites and sea campion, which holds, in its bladder base, mysterious colonies of flies.

Spring is our season of gold. Coltsfoot lifts yellow tassels and celandines spread carpets of stars under the early sun. Great tracts of marsh marigold shine out in swamp and stream. In May we have sunbursts of dandelions along road-verges. The daffodils that line many roadsides are not native, but naturalised after their increase out of bulb bowls into gardens, thence to lawns and roadsides. Primroses, known here as mayflowers, clothe springtime hillsides in pale, greenish-yellow, along with lady's smock, blue-eyed speedwell and blue violets. Wild pansies are sweetly purple in early grain crops and along head-rigs of fields; in Sanday a smaller dune variety grows in hard-packed sand.

Once oatfields were golden with corn marigolds, but these are now less common. Roadsides and churchyards are the habitat of its perennial relative, oxeye daisy, the gowans of *Auld Lang Syne*. Also growing by graveyards and along nearby ditches are the rank rhubarb-like leaves of butter-bur, whose pale-purple flowers rise before its foliage in spring.

June is the flowery month, when Orkney blossoms forth in orchid-purple and mauve, with a multitude of dainty things on moor, shore and bog. Between the heather-bushes creeps milkwort in blue, pink and white; slender, white-flowered purging flax; red-rattle or lousewort; kidney vetch; tormentil; lemon-yellow mouse-eared hawkweed; trefoil; and sometimes, if one lifts a branch of heather, there grows the lesser twayblade, not a spectacular plant but worth finding. Despite its apparent frailty it has an extensive root system. The greater twayblade is a greenish-flowered orchid, rising from roundish twin leaves. The inconspicuous frog orchid and the small white, are rare; the early purple grows in a few places. My favourite, the fragrant *Gymnadenia conopsea*, of which there are two varieties, one more strongly clove-carnation scented than the other, may be nosed before being seen! The handsome northern fen-orchid is the most common, and resembles a hyacinth.

Yellow irises stand stiffly beside watercourses. Tracts of ragged robin glow softly pink over bog-land, where may be found an exquisite tiny plant, bog pimpernel, looking like a pink-flowered moss; and possibly alpine meadow rue, lifting minute flower-heads in its brief season. Here are sundews, and butterwort with its shiny-green starfish leaves and violet-coloured flowers; both of these are insectivorous. On pond-margins we may find bog stitchwort, with delicate white petals; and in moorland, grass of Parnassus, which is not a grass but a low-growing white flower. Mountain everlasting is a common plant of heathland, with fluffy, grey-white flowers.

Tall buttercups shine goldenly over fields, and ragwort makes a bright splash of colour unwelcome to the farmer. Also very lovely is the lemon-yellow wild mustard of cultivated land, which can colour fields so vividly that

Primula Scotica

they gleam out in dusky midnight at midsummer.

A spectacular summer flower is red campion, which varies in shade from deep-rose to pale pink or white. A bright stand of crimson is likely to be rosebay, most handsome and troublesome of willowherbs. Purple foxgloves run up hilldykes in company with tawny-yellow whin.

Wild parsley edges springtime roads in frothy white; hogweed and wild angelica raise tall umbrella heads in summer, and stand dry and brittle throughout the winter.

Travelling along cracks in the rocks of the shore is sea-milkwort, in a delicate tracery of minute pink flowers. We have oysterplant on a few beaches, and sea-bindweed on one. In late summer corn sow-thistles lift great dandelion-like heads on tall stems by seaside and field-margin.

We seldom have autumnal tones on our trees because of the winds that sweep them bare; but moorland and peat-bog copy the shades of the fall in the russet overwintering tones of bog asphodel, and other swampland vegetation which weathers to crimson and dull-gold. The last flowers of the season are devil's bit scabious, which nods blue heads over heath and moor, contrasting with the yellow hawkweeds. But what can be more beautiful, year-long, than the common daisy, star-scattered on the grass?

A Checklist of Vascular Plants, Flowering Plants and Ferns by Elaine R. Bullard, is a comprehensive and invaluable list of Orkney flora which I recommend.

Mammals of Orkney

Sheila Spence

There are just fourteen different species of mammals living in and around the islands, which is about half the number of species found in mainland Britain. At one time the theory put forward to explain the presence of these mammals in Orkney was that their ancestors had been left behind when the retreat of the Ice Age, and the consequent rise in sea level, had caused the islands to be separated from mainland Britain. Today, scientific opinions are that most of the Orkney mammals have been introduced either accidentally or intentionally. Historical and present day records certainly support this theory in the case of some of the Orkney mammals.

Rabbits
Rabbits can be seen on all the islands at any time of the day or night. They

are indistinguishable from those of mainland Britain. They are found on all types of terrain from the heathery slopes of the peat banks, amongst the farmlands, to the sandy links and dunes around the coasts. During the early 1960s, myxomatosis was introduced into Orkney and spread rapidly amongst the rabbit population causing a considerable reduction in their numbers. By the late 1970s, however, numbers had again increased and today rabbits are once again numerous. Myxomatosis is still present in the rabbit population but the disease does not seem to be so acute and some rabbits have been known to recover.

Hares

Two species of hares can be seen in Orkney. The Mountain or Blue hare can be seen only on or near the Cuilags and Ward Hill on the Island of Hoy. This hare, whose coat changes from brown in summer to white in winter, was recorded as being present on Hoy by a writer in the sixteenth century. The other species of hare—the Brown hare—was introduced to Mainland Orkney and the Islands of Hoy, Eday, Rousay, Shapinsay and South Ronaldsay last century to provide sport for the landowners of that time. Now Orkney farms are almost all entirely owner-occupied and hare hunting no longer takes place as before. At the present time the Brown hare remains only on the Orkney Mainland and on the Island of Rousay.

Mice

Although not quite so easy to observe as the rabbits and the hares, two species of mice are present in Orkney. The first, like the rabbit, is present on every island. This is the House mouse and it can be found in town and farm buildings, in dwelling houses, in stacks in the fields, in fact anywhere that man has stores of food that are attractive to mice. With its greyish fur it is similar to the House mouse of mainland Britain but recent detailed scientific studies have shown that these mammals vary from island to island and that the average weight of a mouse from some of the island populations can be almost twice that of a mouse in mainland Britain. The other species of mouse in Orkney is the Wood mouse. To date, it is recorded as being present only on Mainland Orkney and the Islands of Shapinsay, Graemsay, Hoy, Copinsay, Sanday and North Ronaldsay. It is much more timid than the House mouse. It has an orange-brown coat, a white underbelly and a very long tail, which gives it its other name of the Long-tailed Field mouse. It favours grassy banks and ditches for its nest, while the House mouse tends to nest closer to man and his environment. It is perhaps for this reason that the Wood mouse is known locally on North Ronaldsay as the Bank mouse.

Rats

Orkney has two species of rats. The more common one, the Brown rat, can be found on Mainland Orkney and the Islands of Hoy, Graemsay, Rousay, Wyre, Shapinsay, Egilsay, Stronsay and Sanday whilst the Black rat is found only on the Island of Westray. The Black rat is smaller than the Brown rat with a much darker silkier coat, a longer tail and bigger ears. By nature it is less aggressive and in mainland Britain when the two species come into contact the Black rat is usually driven off by the Brown rat. Several centuries ago it was the Black rat that was present in Orkney but as the Brown rat became established the Black rat was slowly driven off. Historians, writing at different periods during last century, recorded the gradual spread of the Brown rat and the decline of the Black rat, the last recorded sighting of the Black rat being on South Ronaldsay in the 1930s. In the year 1939 there were no rats on the Island of Westray but towards the end of that year a German grain boat ran aground just below the farm of Skaill. The Black rats went ashore and, as there were no Brown rats there, they gradually established themselves, and their descendants are still present today.

Pygmy Shrews

The Pygmy shrew, the smallest member of the shrew family, is present in Orkney where it is known as the 'nebbit-moose' (the nosed-mouse). It can be found on Mainland Orkney and the Islands of Hoy, Graemsay, Flotta, Shapinsay, Rousay, Stronsay, Westray and Copinsay. It does not burrow but uses runs constructed by other small mammals in the grass of meadows and burn sides.

Water Shrews

The Water shrew was first recorded on the Island of Hoy last century but the naturalists of that time were very doubtful about accepting the fact. During the 1960s, however, it was once again observed by two visiting naturalists. So far it has not been recorded on any of the other islands. Any observation of this mammal by visitors would be most welcome.

Orkney Voles

The Orkney vole is the only mammal present in Orkney which is not found in mainland Britain. It closely resembles the Short-tailed vole of mainland Britain but it is much bigger and has a variation in its tooth formation. It is found on the Mainland of Orkney and the Islands of Rousay, Westray and Sanday. As it is active during the day, it can often be observed by walkers in grassy meadows, along the banks of burns and on the grassy tops of cliffs. Its colonies consist of a labyrinth of very characteristic runs, built by the voles amongst the grass. These runs are easily spotted, especially in the early spring when the grass is still withered and the new grass not yet grown.

Hedgehogs

Of all the Orkney mammals, the hedgehog is the one that has most recently been introduced and is therefore the best recorded. There is a record from last century of an attempt to introduce hedgehogs to Orkney but nothing seems to have come of it. During the early years of this century the cargo boats *Cormorant* and *Busy Bee* came into Kirkwall every summer with cargoes of fencing stabs from Loch Eriboll. The crews of these boats always brought in hedgehogs which they gave out to the many small boys who spent their summer days around the Kirkwall pier. By the 1950s hedgehogs were frequently seen on the Mainland of Orkney, particularly around the former war time camp of Netherbutton in Holm, and it was suggested that they had been brought in by the great influx of troops and civilian personnel passing in and out of Orkney during the 1939-45 war. A known introduction of hedgehogs was made about 1946 into Holm from the Shetland Isles. They were exchanged for cabbage butterflies which were taken to Shetland where they were unknown at that time. Since then, successful recorded introductions have been made from Mainland Orkney into the islands of Shapinsay, Eday, North Ronaldsay, Westray, Egilsay, Hoy and Flotta. Introductions have also been made into Wyre from Egilsay and Hoy from Stroma and Shetland.

Otters

Contrary to findings in mainland Britain, the otter in Orkney seems to be still quite plentiful. They are found in the burns, lochs and sea and on the shores of all the islands. They are very retiring animals and are most frequently seen by the lone angler or duck shooter out in the early dawn or at dusk. Farmers out quietly observing their animals during early morning or late evening will also tell of seeing a family of otters playing beside a loch or burn. There are no dates recorded for the first appearance of otters in Orkney but from the number of old place names that refer to otters, it is obvious that they have been around for a considerable time.

Seals

The sea around the islands of Orkney is frequented by two species of seals—the Grey seal and the Common seal. Both species can be seen at any time of the year and travellers on the inter-island boats will often see them either in the water or perhaps lying hauled out on the shore. In the water the Grey seal can be distinguished from the Common seal by the shape of its head which is larger, longer, and more horse-like. The Common seal has a rounder more dog-like head. On shore the Grey seal tends to lie with its tail on the ground and with its head and the top part of its body raised, whereas the Common seal often lies with both head and tail raised, giving its outline the typical 'banana' shape. In general, the Grey seal is more numerous in the open waters around the northern isles and the Common seal favours the more sheltered waters of Scapa Flow, though neither species is strictly confined to these areas. July and August are the months when the majority of Common seal pups are born in Orkney waters. A skerry or sand bank, which is exposed only at low tide, is chosen by the mother. On this she gives birth to a single pup and by the time the tide has risen mother and pup are ready to go into the sea where the pup will be suckled. The pups are born with a coat colour similar to the adults. It is not until October that the majority of Grey seal pups are born in Orkney. The Grey seal mother usually selects a very secluded and steep rocky shore on which to give birth to her single pup. Once the pup is born the mother goes back to the sea but remains close at hand within sight and sound of her pup on the shore and hauls out only when it is time to suckle the pup. This pup, which has a white coat when born, grows very rapidly and, after about three weeks it has grown a grey mottled coat, trebled its birth weight and is ready to go out to sea with its mother. From the many references to seals, called *selkies* locally, in the folk tales of Orkney, it would seem that seals have been in this area for a very long time.

Dolphins, Porpoises and Whales

The appearance of the large sea mammals in Orkney waters is only part of the seasonal movement of these creatures through the North Sea and the Atlantic Ocean and sightings are therefore very variable. Dolphins and porpoises seem to follow the shoals of herring and haddock round the North of Scotland, and during the months of July and August they are often seen in the Pentland Firth by travellers on the St. Ola as she makes her daily run from Stromness to Scrabster. Sea anglers and others fishing from small boats, not far off shore, will sometimes be treated to the sight of a school of these mammals swimming around, under and alongside the boat.

Whales, although much rarer than they were in previous centuries, can still be sighted from time to time. Passengers on the St. Ola or on board one of the small planes making inter-island flights may be fortunate enough to see single or sometimes several of these mammals.

From time to time dolphins, porpoises and whales run aground on the island shores and then it is much easier to identify the species, but such strandings are erratic and can in no way be predicted. In previous centuries strandings were more frequent and this fate-sent gift of oil, flesh and whalebone deposited on their shores, was welcomed by the islanders. In fact, schools of whales, spotted close to the island, would often be deliberately driven ashore. The cry of 'whales in the bay' would be the signal for every able-bodied man and boy on the island to stop whatever they were doing and make for the boats. Once the boats had got between the whales and the open sea the occupants would start to make as much noise as possible in order to drive the whales ashore. In contrast, the sight of a school of whales approaching an island at the present day would still cause people to take to the boats but with the intention of driving them out to deeper water.

Birds of Orkney

Eric Meek, R.S.P.B. Orkney Officer

Anyone visiting Orkney for the first time is immediately struck by the sheer numbers of birds which the islands support. The underlying rocks are of a type which produce a relatively rich soil which holds huge numbers of invertebrates and which, in turn maintains a large population of land birds. The surrounding sea is correspondingly rich, lying as it does in an area where comparatively fresh coastal water and more saline oceanic water become mixed. Such conditions are ideal for breeding plankton which attract fish which are, in turn, preyed upon by sea birds.

A visitor in summer will perhaps be first attracted to the sea-cliffs where the horizontal sandstone ledges provide ideal breeding sites for the commoner sea-birds. It is hard to find a cliff anywhere in the islands which does not have its nesting Fulmars and it is hard to believe that these 'mini-albatrosses' have only been present here since the turn of the century. Other species are more localised, but, on those cliffs where they do nest, are often present in large numbers. Marwick Head in north-west Mainland, for example, holds some 25,000 Guillemots, almost 5,000 pairs of Kittiwakes and almost 1000 Razorbills. A colony of similar size can be found on the island of Copinsay lying off the East Mainland with an even larger one on Westray's Noup Cliffs. All three of these sites, which are amongst the most important sea-bird colonies in Britain, are reserves of the Royal Society for the Protection of Birds. Many sea-birds do not nest on cliffs but prefer the inland moors or the unique areas of gently undulating maritime heath as found, for example, on the North Hill of Papa Westray or in the Quandale-Brings area of north-west Rousay. In such situations can be found vast colonies of Arctic Terns, one of the hardiest of ocean wanderers which completes a round trip of some 15,000 miles each year on its journeys between its northern breeding grounds and its wintering areas in the Southern Ocean. Those master-pirates, the Arctic Skuas, also nest in such habitat and harass the terns in spectacular aerial combat until the fish carried by the latter are dropped in fright; the skua then swoops down catching its purloined meal before it hits the sea! The larger Great Skua, or Bonxie, is present only in small numbers on the Mainland and North Isles but is much more plentiful on the high moors of Hoy where, during a summer walk, you must always be prepared to take evasive action as these bulky individuals hurtle at your head in defence of their eggs or young.

It is difficult to imagine that Orkney's sea-birds, present as they are in such enormous numbers, could ever be threatened; but the threats are there. The development of oil-related activities in the islands has brought with it the ever-present danger of oil-pollution. In recent years oiling incidents have been thankfully few but constant vigilance is needed. The other insidious threat is the development of factory-fishing which involves the scooping up of enormous quantities of small fish such as Sand-eels which form the main prey of many sea-birds. How far can the depletion of fish stocks go before the birds begin to feel the effects?

The heather moorlands of Orkney support a unique community of heathland birds. Chief amongst these is the Hen Harrier whose slow, flapping flight belies the efficiency with which it hunts Orkney Voles and young Rabbits. With almost 100 nests in a good year, Orkney may hold up to 20 per cent of the British population of this scarce bird of prey. The beautiful grey males are not as common as the brown females and these unequal numbers lead to the males being polygamous, each having two, three and, on occasions, up to seven wives! Other predators dependent on the Orkney Vole as a source of food are the Short-eared Owl, drifting over the heather even more slowly

60

and silently than the Harriers, and the Kestrel which here, in contrast to elsewhere in their range, are able to nest on the ground due to the lack of ground predators such as Foxes, Stoats and Weasels. A close relative of the Kestrel, the Merlin, although similar in appearance, presents a complete contrast in its style of hunting. Rather than hovering in search of voles, the Merlin depends on its speed and agility to catch Meadow Pipits and Skylarks, the two commonest small birds of the moors. Many species of waders also nest on the moors. The commonest is the Curlew (up to 100 pairs breed on the 1875 acre R.S.P.B. reserve at Hobbister) but smaller numbers of Golden Plovers and Dunlins are also present. The small hill-top lochans attract various ducks including Wigeon but are of prime importance for their breeding Red-throated Divers. The divers feed on the nearby sea and their flights to and from the lochans are accompanied by their wild goose-like cries.

Once again it is perhaps difficult for the first-time visitor to envisage any threat to Orkney's moorland birds. However, as a result of agricultural reclamation, the moorlands are continually being nibbled away and, with improving technology the day cannot be far off when the decreasing area of this habitat will begin to make itself felt upon the birds dependent on it.

Another type of habitat which has declined in area is marshland. As a result of drainage comparatively few wetlands now remain in Orkney in common with the situation in the rest of the country. Sanday, Stronsay and North Ronaldsay still retain some good examples while on the Mainland the best marsh left is at The Loons in Birsay. Now mostly protected by R.S.P.B. reserve status this extremely rich area holds no fewer than nine species of breeding ducks and seven species of breeding waders as well as substantial colonies of Common and Black-headed Gulls and Arctic Terns. Amongst the ducks, in 1981, were nine pairs of Pintails, a species with fewer than fifty pairs nesting in Britain. With that fast-declining ventriloquist, the Corncrake, occasionally nesting in its drier margins, The Loons provide an insight into what many other parts of Orkney must have been like in the past.

In winter the visitor to Orkney may have to work a little harder for his birds but the impression is still of large numbers. Flocks of Common Gulls, Lapwings and Curlews stalk the fields, enormous flocks of wildfowl from northern Europe inhabit the larger lochs, especially Harray, and Long-tailed Ducks, Great Northern Divers, Red-breasted Mergansers and Slavonian Grebes make the sea an exciting place to scan with your binoculars. During the migration periods, in spring and autumn, the islands act as stepping-stones for birds such as geese *en route* to and from north-westerly breeding grounds in Iceland and Greenland. In addition, they act as a welcome haven for birds lost during their migratory flights, especially those Continental species drifted across the North Sea by easterly winds. Under these conditions some of the rarest species appear and some of the most anomalous situations occur; on one occasion in September 1982, for example, a Scarlet Rosefinch from Russia and Scandinavia was watched being chased through the tree-tops by a Tennessee Warbler from North America! while in June 1988 a Pallas's Rosefinch from central Siberia, the first ever seen in Britain, was found on North Ronaldsay.

Fishing for Sport

W.E. Knight

TROUT FISHING

Orkney has much to offer the visiting angler. There are six well-stocked lochs—all very accessible. Fishing is free but one must remember that much of the land belongs to local farmers and it is important to ask permission before entering private property. It is also advisable for visitors to join the Orkney Trout Fishing Association. S.A.E. to Mr. S. Headley, Quoys, Stenness, Orkney (Tel. 0856 850077). For a modest fee one gets the benefit of the use of fishing huts on four of the lochs, with car parking on the edge of the loch.

Loch Stenness is a huge loch connected to the sea by a narrow inlet. The water is brackish and its native trout *Salmo orcadensis* seems to be a cross between a sea trout *Salmo trutta* and a brown trout *Salmo fario*. Their flesh is very deep pink and they are bonnie fighters. There is a cast of a monster 29lb. trout caught in this loch. Stenness is unique in that sea fish can be taken as well as trout. During spring tides Saithe (Coley), Pollock, Herring and Plaice sometimes enter the loch, and in 1982 a wading angler netted a 19lb. Turbot.

Loch Harray is another big loch with many miles of shore line to wade, but there are plenty of boats for hire. It is connected to Loch Stenness so one gets sea trout as well as the beautifully marked Harray fish. A normal basket will average 12oz. but on a good day fish of 2-3lb. are common. A few years ago one lucky angler landed a 17lb. beauty. Best flies are *Soldier Palmer, Woodcock and Yellow, Peter Ross* and one of the *Teals*, but a visit to the tackle dealer will tell you the fly doing best at the time.

Lochs Boardhouse, Hundland and Swanney contain the real brown trout. The waters are peaty and the fish are great fighters. They bore to the bottom when hooked so that you never see the fish until it is brought to net. Boardhouse is a fine loch for boat fishing and the middle drift often yields a good basket when the shore drift proves unproductive. Hundland is an interesting small loch well worth a visit. It should be waded as there are submerged reefs all through the loch. Loch Swanney is very popular with local anglers because of the quality of the fish. One seldom gets a big basket in numbers but fish of 3-4lb. are common. Favoured flies are the local *Ke-He, Black Zulu, Greenwell, Bluebottle, Invicta* and on a breezy day the *Loch Ordie* does well.

Loch Kirbister is the only loch on the south side of the Mainland. The fish tend to be smaller than those in the other lochs, but can provide a lively session when a rise is on.

Sea trout come into the bays around the coast from July onwards. A *Teal* and *Red Terror* or a mackerel strip are the favourite lures.

Given reasonable weather the visiting angler will return to the South with memories of quiet lochs disturbed only by the plop of a fish or the song of the birds.

SEA ANGLING

Sea angling is a comparatively new sport in Orkney. There is good fishing all round the coast and some superb specimens have been landed. A 212lb. Common Skate broke a fifty-six year old British record and a 161lb. Halibut was the first fish over 100lb. to be taken on rod and line.

Most anglers visiting Orkney for the first time arrive with tackle too light for the conditions. Currents are strong and the best fish lie on rocky bottom. Minimum bottom weight should be 12oz. but, in deep water and spring tides up to 2lb. is used. Fishing is carried out on the drift and it is essential that line is retrieved quickly when sounding bottom.

Stromness is the main centre for fishing, but Kirkwall, St. Margaret's Hope and Longhope are near good fishing grounds. The Northern Isles could provide the best fishing of all, and the angler lucky enough to get a day out with the local fishermen could break new records. Individual anglers may find it difficult to get a place in a boat. It would be best to come in a party of six to ten and book a boat in advance. Beach casting is not practised much but Plaice and Flounders can be taken from sandy beaches and there are rocks where Saithe and Pollock are plentiful. The visitor should seek local advice before venturing to fish from the rocks as some can be dangerous when a ground swell is running. The Churchill Barriers are also popular with shore anglers and reasonable catches of Codling and Saithe can sometimes be taken.

The coastline of Orkney provides scenery which can best be appreciated from a boat. The majesty of the 1160ft. sheer cliffs of St. John's Head in Hoy makes the angler feel very insignificant, and one should always salute the Old Man of Hoy when in the vicinity. Elsewhere the cliffs are alive with nesting seabirds and the seas around are a constant source of entertainment with the antics of Puffins, Razorbills, Guillemots and Fulmars.

In the 1982 Orkney Open Boat Championships fifty-eight anglers weighed in over 7000lb. of fish, with Ling to 37lb., Cod to 18lb., and a British record Tusk of 15lb. 7oz. In another festival a few years ago, Halibut of 170lb. and 180lb. were landed on successive days.

Further information can be obtained by sending a S.A.E. to Mr. J.R. Geddes, Secretary, Orkney Sea Angling Association, Quarryfield, Orphir, Orkney (Tel. 0856 81311).

The Arts in Orkney

Erlend Brown, Curator, The Pier Arts Centre, Stromness

Orkney, for its size and population, has much to offer in cultural activity. The museums are rich in artefacts of Orkney's heritage. Indeed, with the growing interest in ancient cultures, and the proliferation of prehistoric sites throughout the islands, Orkney offers 5,000 years of artistic development.

But what of recent activity in the arts? Literature, music, drama, dance, the fine and applied arts are all practised to a greater or lesser extent.

Three major writers of creative imagination have emerged in the twentieth century in Orkney. Edwin Muir (1887-1959) poet, critic, translator, is an important writer by any standards. His childhood on the small north isle of Wyre had a lasting impression on his work. George Mackay Brown says of Muir, 'His poetry has the profundity and visionary quality of myth—it seems to tap deep unapprehended sources, going back countless generations to the very roots.' George Mackay Brown is still actively involved, on a full-time basis, in the craft of writing. His poetry, prose and occasional dramatic pieces, owe a lot to the story-telling oral tradition that goes as far back as *The Orkneyinga Saga.*

Another honoured son is Eric Linklater (1889-1974). There is a largeness and vigour in his novels which could also be said to go back in spirit to the saga men.

Orkney Press promotes the work of younger writers in Orkney. It is to their credit that local writers of imagination and local knowledge have had their works published in the past few years. We are also fortunate that the local lore of the islands has been collected in the book *Folklore of Orkney and*

Shetland by Ernest W. Marwick (1915-1977).

Musical education has improved immeasurably in the last twenty years. Not only in schools, but through Orkney Arts Society, performances of quality can be heard in many venues—St. Magnus Cathedral, Orkney Arts Theatre, Orkney schools and Stromness Town Hall. The latter venue houses a marvellous grand piano and hosts a lively summer school of music.

A Scottish influence is apparent in the Strathspey and Reel Societies in Kirkwall and Stromness, but Ronnie Aim and others have composed works for fiddle and accordion and Ally Windwick has composed some excellent songs. Shetland may be more associated with a fiddle playing tradition, but it cannot be said to be lacking in Orkney. The accordion is also a popular instrument. A weekend Folk Festival occurs in late May. Locally based talent along with professional musicians from the south are mainly based in Stromness, but also take part in community events throughout Orkney mainland and the outer isles. The St. Magnus Festival, a celebration of new music and local performance, is a highlight of mid-summer in Orkney. From its beginning in the mid-seventies, the musical emphasis has broadened to include drama, poetry and prose (*A Johnsmas Foy*) and various exhibitions. The composer, Peter Maxwell Davies, is the artistic director of the Festival. Living part of the year in Orkney has led him to compose new works. Some of the liveliest and perhaps most accessible, have been works especially written for Orkney schoolchildren—*Kirkwall Shopping Songs, Cinderella, The Rainbow* and *Hoy Songs.*

The Orkney Arts Theatre in Kirkwall (seats 300) has added greatly to the provision of the performing arts in Orkney. An annual pantomine is always a sell-out before Christmas. The Operatic Society puts on a light opera in mid-February and at the end of that month the local Scottish Community Drama Association's One-Act Play Festival attracts teams from all over mainland Orkney and the outer isles. All play to packed audiences and a spirited participation is always assured.

The disciplines of painting, sculpture, film-making and photography have all had their devotees over the last fifty years. Stanley Cursiter was the Queen's Limner in Scotland. As director of the Scottish National Galleries he also built up a reputation as a fine portrait painter. But there was nothing he loved better than to return to paint the many moods of landscape in his native Orkney. Ian MacInnes and Sylvia Wishart have responded to the Orkney landscape in very different ways. Ian Scott, the North Ronaldsay sculptor, uses sea forms as a continuing theme. Indeed, there has been a flowering of new talent over the last ten years. This is, in many respects, due to the founding of the Pier Arts Centre in Stromness in 1979. The buildings house a permanent collection of twentieth century British paintings and sculptures given to Orkney by Margaret Gardiner. There are fine examples of work by Ben Nicholson, Barbara Hepworth, Naum Gabo and Eduardo Paolozzi. There is also a programme of temporary exhibitions which includes an open week, where any work submitted will go on show. Children's artwork and exhibitions of works by professional painters, sculptors and photographers, lectures, poetry readings, films and other small scale events also feature. The Ballroom Gallery and Shorelines Gallery in Kirkwall also promote work by local artists.

The films of Margaret Tait are unique in Orkney. She is an independent film maker producing very good work on a limited budget. *Landmakar*, a recent film, was very well received by Orcadians.

There has also been a flowering of the applied arts in Orkney encouraged by the Orkney Craftsmans Guild. Two silvercraft units are among the main producers in the U.K., employing over fifty people and exporting world-wide. Top quality and high fashion knitwear is much sought after by international buyers. Potters, furniture makers, woodcarvers and leather workers have all established themselves in a competative market. Traditional arts and crafts are maintained while modern designs and techniques are explored to the full.